GANDHI
Going to Wipe their Tears

By Pyarelal Nayar

Compiled by
Mahendra Meghani

MapinLit
AN IMPRINT OF
MAPIN PUBLISHING

First published in India in 2002 by
Navajivan Trust, Ahmedabad 380014

Reprinted in 2008 with the permission of
Navajivan Trust
by MapinLit
An imprint of
Mapin Publishing

Mapin Publishing Pvt. Ltd.
10B Vidyanagar Society Part I
Usmanpura, Ahmedabad 380014
T: 91 79 2754 5390/91 • F: 2754 5392
E: mapin@mapinpub.com • www.mapinpub.com

Text © Navajivan Trust
Front Jacket Illustration by Snehal Chitlange

ISBN: 978-81-88204-87-8 (Mapin)
ISBN: 978-1-890206-26-0 (Grantha)

Designed by Snehal Chitlange/Mapin Design Studio
Printed in India

CONTENTS

EQUITY OF LIBERATION:
A GANDHIAN EFFORT

Systems have changed through the centuries, but need and the realization of need designed through apt implementation have never been better understood by anyone but Gandhi. The ease with which Gandhi brought self-reliance, truth, and non-violence into common practice in the Indian society depicts that his method was effective enough to establish a continual command upon the mental plane of the following generations. After a long lacuna of centuries, Gandhi was born to become the symbol of the universe of creativity. His message towards a utopian society is a purgative experiment on one's own self. In fact, the whole battle for independence was fought and won following Gandhi's knowledge of human demands.

The social creativity of Mahatma Gandhi revealed a concrete, genuine human path of love, through his life of spiritual and existential combat for human rights for the whole humanity. The outward simplicity of his life and his single-minded devotion to non-violence cloaked innumerable deep currents of ideas, disciplines, loyalties and aspirations. There was nothing mystical or miraculous about his development and growth from a common man into the unsurpassed Mahatma of our history. This was the base of the popular acceptance of his knowledge system.

The present book, apart from being a historical document of India's strife for communal harmony, also serves to establish Gandhi as a unique propounder of the equity of liberation. Gandhian thought is all the more contemporary nowadays. Gandhi demonstrated that the practice of non-violent social action could transform self-hatred into self-love, and could move the oppressor from violence to empathy and compassion. Gandhi, an authentic liberation psychologist, embodied in his social creativity model the virtues of kindness, selflessness, civility, firmness, courage, lawfulness, self-mastery, love, and Truth.

The famous followers of the Gandhian thought of liberation have fought great battles for social or political justice, using the principles of Mahatma Gandhi. Five amongst them stand out strongly: Martin Luther King, Nelson Mandela, the Dalai Lama, Aung San Suu Kyi and César Chávez, who struggled to reduce the exploitation of farm workers in California. Three of these—Mandela, the Dalai Lama and Suu Kyi—have been awarded the Nobel Prize for Peace. All proudly acknowledge their debt to Gandhi.

No other knowledge system has been as simple and creative as the Gandhian one, in moulding the ever-youthful minds for generations, to give them the opportunity to become fully functioning, self-actualized and self-realized individuals. What Gandhi developed is an indigenous doctrine of knowledge which has the strength of reaching unto the last in its simplest form and which drafted an everlasting bio-political system which remains a credible alternative to common beliefs and faiths, and which is much more humane, practical and down to earth in the creation of a universal society.

Dr Neerja Arun

INTRODUCTION

The present book covers the last years of Mahatma Gandhi's life, in which the results of all the experiments that he carried out throughout his career were put to final test. The author's writings in *Young India* and *Harijan* and several works on Mahatma Gandhi have well established him as a faithful and authoritative chronicler and interpreter of Gandhiji's life and philosophy.

It is only in a detailed account of what Gandhiji did, how and why he did it, that a soul-stirring picture of his life and teaching can be found. The present work represents such an attempt by one who had first-hand knowledge of the events he has described and has the insight to interpret them correctly.

What made Mahatma Gandhi almost unique among leaders was his capacity to harmonize widely different points of view so that they became contributory to the prosecution of the common goal. An outstanding instance was the way in which he dealt with his colleagues in the Congress organization who differed from him. While holding to his own principle, he allowed his colleagues full scope to serve the country according to their light. As a result of this, not only did most intimate relations continue between them, but also those who differed from him ultimately came round and worked under his leadership.

Gandhiji was uncompromisingly opposed to the Partition of India, which he had called her vivisection. The Muslim League agitation for the Partition of the country resulted in serious rioting. Partition, based on a wrong theory and brought about by such questionable means, Gandhiji was certain, would do irretrievable harm to both Hindus and Muslims—in India and Pakistan. But he left it to the Congress Ministers in the Central Government, who were in charge of running the administration, to act according to their judgment. Once they had decided in favour of Partition, he did not oppose them, although he never concealed his own opinion. Instead of carrying on propaganda against his own colleagues, he set about with an amazing energy to repair the vast damage to communal harmony and peace which preceded and followed the Partition. His words became commands, his mere presence sometimes sufficed to check the blaze where the police and army could have succeeded only after much bloodshed.

It is this last phase of his life which is particularly dealt with in this book with insight, understanding and restraint, and with meticulous regard for accuracy. Some of the most fascinating pages of the book are devoted to describing the functioning of his mind in search of new techniques for setting India on the road to the new social order of his dreams. The time had arrived when, with all the experience and prestige acquired in the course of the Indian struggle for freedom which he had conducted for more than 30 years, Mahatma Gandhi could extend the ambit of his activities and prove that ahimsa could work wonders even in the most adverse of circumstances. At this stage he was taken away. But the ideas and forces he has released may yet accomplish things even more marvellous than were witnessed in his lifetime.

The core of Gandhiji's teaching was meant for all mankind and is valid for all time. He wanted all men to be free so that they would grow unhampered into full self-realization. He wanted to abolish the exploitation of man by man in any form, because both exploitation and submission to it are a sin against the law of our being. He had been invited by many foreigners to visit their countries and deliver his message to them directly. But he had declined since, as he said, he must make good what he claimed for Truth and Ahimsa in his own country before he could launch on the gigantic task of converting the world. With the attainment of freedom by India by following his method, in spite of all the imperfections in its practice, the condition precedent for taking his message to other countries was to a certain extent fulfilled. And he might have been able to turn his attention to this larger question. But Providence had ordained otherwise. May some individual or nation arise and carry forward the effort launched by him.

Rajendra Prasad

PREFACE

The Last Phase presents a full, detailed and authentic story of the ultimate phase of Gandhiji's life, in which his spiritual dynamism was at the height of its power. The book deals with the period from his release from detention in the Aga Khan's Palace, in 1944, up to the end of his life.

An amazing story of the mingling of streams of Eastern and Western thought from which he derived his spiritual nourishment, and a meteoric rise to recognition and fame unfolds to a student of Gandhiji's life. A shrinking, shy, immature youth, unsure of himself and baffled by life's jigsaw puzzle, he finds himself—an utter stranger in a strange land, where a freak of fortune had thrown him—suddenly confronted by the challenge of racial and political prejudice at its worst. Armed with nothing save unsoiled integrity, undeterred by fear of where it might lead him, he takes up that challenge, and in the short span of two years becomes a factor to be reckoned with. Practically single-handed, he changes the course of political events, inspiring many with awe and even affection. Whence came this strength and what was the secret of his alchemy?

His capacity for compromise—rooted in the habit he had cultivated of seeing a problem from the opponent's viewpoint—and for trust which begets trust, enabled him to win the respect and goodwill even of those with whom he was locked in a fierce conflict and to convert determined antagonists into personal friends.

The transformation in South Africa was due almost entirely to the unremitting toil of one man, member of a despised race, with no official status or authority, save what his selfless service and the moral pressure generated by it gave him—MK Gandhi, the Mahatma-to-be.

Gandhiji's work in South Africa can be properly studied only as a prelude to India's struggle for independence. No better apprenticeship for it could have been found than what South Africa provided. There, he had to raise from the dust a people who had come to regard insults and humiliations in pursuit of a living as their lot, who were torn by dissensions and divided into factions. The authorities were only too eager to exploit their differences. In short, every one of the problems that Gandhiji had to tackle later, in the course of India's non-violent struggle, had its prototype in this microcosm of South Africa. All this experience proved to be a most valuable asset to him in his confrontation with the British Empire during India's fight for liberation. None of his Indian colleagues in the struggle had the advantage of this vast and varied experience.

*

What I have drawn upon, in the first instance, are Gandhiji's office records, his own writings in *Young India* and *Harijan*, statements to the press and personal correspondence. I had, besides, my own notebooks and diaries, as well as notebooks of other members of the party. I have relied upon his own journal which he began specially for me—to make up for my absence from him at the time of the second Simla Conference in May, 1946—and which was continued till July, 1947.

In giving quotations from Gandhiji's speeches and interviews, I have taken the liberty to amplify or revise the language of the published version with the help of the original notes. I have spared no pains to check up and verify information by reference to the actors in the drama. In support of my conclusions, I have cited appropriate chapter and verse; hence the close documentation which has added to the bulk of the volume.

I have, in some cases, departed from the dates and sequence of events, relating to certain incidents in Gandhiji's career as given in his own writings. In every such case, I have fully justified my reasons with evidence. I have also taken the liberty in some places to give my own translation of some of the quotations from Gandhiji's *Autobiography*, originally in Gujarati, where I felt that the corresponding version given in *The Story of My Experiments with Truth* was either faulty or not sufficiently clear.

*

Almost the first thing a foreign visitor does on arrival in India is to visit Rajghat, to pay homage to the Father of the Nation. Before he leaves, he invariably ends up asking: "Where is Gandhi in the India of today?" That is a question which every one of us owes to himself, to the India for whom Gandhiji lived and died, and to the world, to ask and answer. This book is an attempt to help us turn the searchlight inward and find the answer.

Pyarelal

[Compiled from "Introductions" to Vols 1 and 2 of *Mahatma Gandhi: The Early Phase* and *The Discovery of Satyagraha*.]

THE EDITOR'S NOTE

This is how Pyarelal, secretary to Gandhiji, reminisces about his brief separation from the master during the last months of the Mahatma's life:

On the 20th November, 1946, Gandhiji broke up his camp and accompanied only by his stenographer and Professor Nirmal Kumar Bose, his Bengali interpreter, set out Columbus-like to face the dark unknown. Many voices were husky, many eyes dim with tears as the tiny bamboo country-craft bearing him passed under the arches of the Ramgunj bridge and disappeared in the distance in the direction of Srirampur. In a statement, he said:

"I find myself in the midst of exaggeration and falsity. I am unable to discover the truth. Truth and Ahimsa by which I swear, and which have sustained me for sixty years, seem to fail to show the attributes I have ascribed to them. To test them, or better to test myself, I am going to a village called Srirampur, cutting myself away from those who have been with me all these years. They will each distribute themselves in villages of Noakhali to do the work of peace between the two communities.

"I have decided to suspend all other activities in the shape of correspondence, including the heavy work of *Harijan* and the allied weeklies.

"Ahimsa for me is the chief glory of Hinduism. I hold that India has to demonstrate it to the world. Do I represent this Ahimsa in my person? It is only by going into isolation from my companions, those on whose help I have relied all along, and standing on my own crutches that I shall find my bearings and also test my faith in God."

A few days later, in a letter, he wrote:
"My present mission is the most complicated and difficult one of my life. I can sing (with Cardinal Newman): 'The night is dark and I am far from home, Lead Thou me on.' I never experienced such

darkness in my life before. The night seems long. The only consolation is that I feel neither baffled nor disappointed. 'Do or Die' has to be put to test here. 'Do' here means that Hindus and Muslims should learn to live together in peace and amity. Otherwise, I should die in the attempt. God's will be done."

*

Ever since his departure from Noakhali in the first week of March, 1947, Gandhiji had constantly been in touch with his co-workers in Noakhali. To him, Noakhali and Bihar still held the key to India's future. That was why he was so anxious to get back there as early as possible. In one of his letters to me he wrote: "It fills me with joy to read the accounts of your work. I would like to fly to you. But Kashmir calls me."

I gave him the latest news on Noakhali. This led to a discussion on Noakhali.

Referring to some of the experiments in constructive non-violence that I had been conducting in Noakhali, and some of which, at his bidding, I had recorded in *Harijan*, he proceeded. "How I have longed to do all these things myself! What we need is to shed the fear of death and steal into the hearts and affections of those we serve. This you have done. To love, you have joined knowledge and diligence. Forget others. If even one person—you alone, for instance—did one's part fully and well, it would cover all."

He then outlined to me the plan of his proposed visit to Pakistan and said: "You can go to Noakhali, disengage yourself and return in time to accompany me to Pakistan."

*

As I gazed at the still sad face, infinite peace, forgiveness, and compassion writ large on it, the entire vista of twenty-eight long years of close, unbroken association—from the time when, fresh from the college, I had come to him, full of dazzling dreams and undimmed hopes, and sat at his feet—flashed across the mind's eye.

*

The above passages from Pyarelal's monumental work *Mahatma Gandhi: The Last Phase* give us glimpses of the stray contacts he was able to maintain with Gandhiji during those months. Gandhiji said: "I have told you, I need you with me. By [your] being away from me, I have missed a lot. There is much I would have liked to share with the world, but I could not because I had left you behind in Noakhali." As we read these words, we realize further the poignancy of the sacrifices Gandhiji made when he "set out Columbus-like to face the dark unknown" in Noakhali, as well as the immensity of the loss of our world with which Gandhiji would have liked to share so much.

But then, as we gather up courage to wade through the pages of *The Last Phase*, we feel deeply grateful to Pyarelal that he strove so wonderfully to make good a great part of our loss. We can imagine how he must have made his mentor in heaven ever more proud of the young collegian, full of dazzling dreams, who had come and sat at his feet back in 1920. Also there, Pyarelal's senior colleague, Mahadev Desai, must also have been gratified to see in the ten volumes of *Mahatma Gandhi* a fair substitute for what he himself was destined to leave for posterity, had he not departed from the world as early as 1942.

*

The Last Phase deals with the last 21 months of Gandhiji's life, beginning with his release from detention in the Aga Khan's Palace, in May, 1944. It describes in fair detail the political developments of those years, resulting from the British Government's intention to relinquish power in India. But the most memorable part of the book portrays the heart-rending communal divide across the sub-continent and Mahatma Gandhi's valiant, single-handed struggle to stand against the tornado of primitive passions. With what super-human strength did Gandhiji carry on the battle is summed up by Pyarelal in one panoramic stroke of the pen: "During those fateful days, like a Titan he rushed from one danger spot to another to prop up the crumbling heavens."

It is Pyarelal's epic story of those days in 1946–47 that I have tried to condense here. That story has become significant as required reading for all of us in the year 2002, because the same ghastly communal conflagration of 55 years ago stares us in the face today. We may recall from the book a letter sent to Gandhiji in Noakhali, written by Dr Syed Mahmud, a Minister in the Congress Government of Bihar, in 1946.

His words ring so pathetically prophetic now:

"I tell the Indian Muslims that if they do not settle the communal question in your lifetime, it will never be settled. That opportunity seems almost to have slipped by. But maybe," he added, "even now if you come, the Hindus might be brought to repentance and the situation still saved." Thereupon Gandhiji, leaving his mission in Noakhali incomplete, went to Bihar. From what he saw there he was compelled to declare: "Shameful things had happened in Noakhali, but the way they were said to have butchered children and even old women in Bihar, and the scale on which they had done it, had far eclipsed Noakhali. Did they want to reduce religion to a competition in beastliness?"

Moreover, Dr Rajendra Prasad, a great leader respected by Muslims and Hindus alike, confessed to him that genuine repentance was lacking among the Hindus. The gloom in Gandhiji's heart deepened and his grief was thus poured out:

"It was cowardice to believe that barbarity such as India had of late witnessed could ever protect a people's culture, religion or freedom." He made bold to say that, wherever there had been such cruelty of late, it had its origin in cowardice, and cowardice never redeemed an individual or a nation.

Five and a half decades later, our country is confronted today with the same cruelty and barbarity rooted in the same fear and cowardice. One can only pray that Pyarelal's labours in recapturing the past may induce us to introspect and may inspire us to act in the present.

*

The Last Phase also forcefully underlines another issue that remains most relevant today—the attitude of the Indian Muslims. Pyarelal describes it in simple, clear words:

Partition had left nearly 40 million Muslims in the Indian Union. The bulk of them had, under the Muslim League's propaganda, given their active or passive support to the division of India. The top Muslim League leaders had since migrated to Pakistan, leaving the rank and file of their coreligionists in a quandary—a confused, demoralized, leaderless mass, without a clearly defined goal. Their emotional loyalty was still with the League. But the essential condition of their existence in India as equal citizens was unreserved loyalty to the Indian Union. They all felt unhappy, bitterly disillusioned.

Eager always to champion the cause of the underdog and to identify himself with the down and out, Gandhiji set himself to put heart into the Indian Muslims. They had to be helped to recognize themselves, rid themselves of the canker of divided loyalty and regain their integrity, dignity and self-respect so that they might legitimately take pride in being the nationals of free India on a footing of equality with the rest in every respect.

Thus, like a wise friend and guide, he missed no opportunity to restore to the Indian Muslims their lost fibre, while bringing home to them their errors which they had to live down and from the consequence of which there was no escape.

In the grim battle that the Indian Union was fighting against the forces of communal fanaticism to make India safe for the minorities and ensure to the minorities their full rights as Indian nationals, they must courageously come out on the side of right and justice and speak out their mind to Pakistan.

Gandhiji had been telling the Muslims that if they continued to sit on the fence instead of courageously denouncing the excesses of their coreligionists and failed to align themselves with the victims of the same even at the risk of their lives, or if they harboured secret sympathy with the perpetrators of those excesses, it would bring down upon them the wrath of those with whom—Pakistan or no Pakistan—the bulk of them must live.

*

The Last Phase alone, out of Pyarelal's ten-volume Mahatma Gandhi, was translated into Gujarati in 1971. During the nerve-shattering days that followed February 27th, 2002 in Gujarat, I happened to leaf through its 2200-odd pages. Any reader would be struck with the great similarities between Gujarat then and Calcutta, Noakhali, Bihar and Delhi in 1946–47. The problems that make us feel so utterly helpless now were the same Gandhiji faced then. Deeply absorbed, we watch breathlessly how delicately but unflinchingly Gandhiji walked barefoot across endless fields sown with the dragon's teeth. Pyarelal paints the glorious scene with only a few unembellished words:

This disc of the rising sun had just begun to peer above the horizon when he set out on his journey with the singing of Poet Tagore's celebrated song:

Walk alone. . .
If they do not hold up the light
When the night is troubled with storm,
O thou of evil luck,
with the thunder-flame of pain ignite thine own heart
and let it burn alone.

The route lay through a landscape of enchanting beauty. A narrow, winding footpath, over which two persons could hardly walk abreast, wound sinuously through colonnades of stately palms, whose straight growing stems and drooping branches were reflected in the glassy surface of the tanks by the side of which they grew.

The reader will be enchanted by Pyarelal's numerous similar descriptions of nature no less than by his subtle analysis of human emotions. One could go on and on quoting examples.

*

Condensing from *Poornahuti*, as the translator Manibhai Desai has most appropriately named the Gujarati version of *The Last Phase*— the story of the final months of Gandhiji's life—into a mere 150 pages I sought to place it before the people of Gujarat. It seemed as if such a book's hour had come and it sold over 10,000 copies in about three months. A good deal of the credit for this goes to the Navjivan Trust, which heavily subsidized the publication at the incredibly low price of Rs 10 instead of Rs 70 at the current rate.

That led me to undertake a similar condensation of the original in English. The task was taken up with a feeling of deep reverence for the Mahatma and respect for his son-like biographer. It is my humble hope that this labour of love may be found of relevant by readers beyond Gujarat and even outside India.

Apart from condensing Dr Rajendra Prasad's preface, I have compiled an introduction from Pyarelal's remarks in *The Last Phase* as well as *The Early Phase*. In all humility, I have ventured to present a collage of patches from various pages of the book to make up a comprehensive portrait of Gandhiji.

Besides correcting obvious misprints, I have changed some words and chapter titles so as to make the condensation worthy of its lofty subject. I am grateful to the Navjivan Trust for their permission to undertake this condensation. I must also thank the friends at the Navjivan Press for putting up with various changes I kept making at the proofreading stage. Prose, they say, is "never done". It holds true even when it is the prose of a craftsman like the author of *The Last Phase*.

I should like to close, if I may, by recalling the words of the one whom even the Mahatma described as his mentor:

"A purer, a nobler, a braver and a more exalted spirit has never moved on this earth. In him Indian humanity at the present time has really reached its high water-mark."

Dr S Radhakrishnan put this quotation at the end of his preface to *Mahatma Gandhi: The Early Phase* in 1965, and added: "These memorable words of GK Gokhale, which he spoke in 1912, have been confirmed by a lifetime of dedication and sacrifice."

Mahendra Meghani

THE TORNADO AND THE TITAN:
A COLLAGE

In Gandhiji, the prophet and the practical statesman met. While the prophet had the vision of the ultimate, the statesman was eyeing upon the immediate. As a statesman, he provided solutions for the current problems and evolved as an exemplary general who led the hosts to victory. As a prophet, he became the "voice in the wilderness", biding his time.

*

Never had Gandhiji reacted as poignantly to great advantage when he had to exhibit his convictions as during those fateful days of 1946–47—like a Titan he rushed from one danger spot to another, ranging from Calcutta, East Bengal, Bihar, Delhi, and anywhere at any given time, to prop up the crumbling heavens. Anything and everything that he did became commands and watchwords for the day: his utterances at the daily prayer meetings, his simple "yes" and "no" gestures, even his silences were rendered meaningful, to bring the frail ship of India's Independence safely to port through the storm-tossed waters that lay ahead.

Thanks to his regular habits, abstemious living, self-discipline, detachment and poise, Gandhiji's body was extremely fit, wiry and resilient, the various faculties and organs intact and functioning to perfection (even during the last days of his life). He had absolute command over sleep. His memory betrayed him at times, sign of flagging, but the mind was razor-sharp, vigorous and quick; the judgement uncannily sure; and the intuitions, if anything, more unerring than ever. At the age of 78, he could still put in an amazing amount of physical and concentrated mental work. He was at the height of his spiritual powers and prestige at home and abroad.

After Independence, in December 1947, when all his friends and colleagues were holding positions of power and prestige in the Government, when the Indian capital was reeling in pomp and pageantry, Gandhiji opted for spiritual solitude, in which he would be surrounded only by his loving friends, isolated from his surroundings and from almost everyone else from the power sector. Through an almost superhuman effort of the will, he was able to preserve his balance and even his good humour in the midst of all this. Whoever came to him was given full attention, serenity and sweetness, the usual sunshine of his humour. He seemed to have access to some hidden reservoir of strength, optimism, joy and peace, which was never affected by the outer circumstances and was transfused to everyone who came in contact with him. Often, veteran freedom fighters came to him bearing grave, careworn faces and heads bent under the load they carried. But when they left, it was with a light heart and a bright countenance, as if they had left all their cares and worries behind, with this perennially young old man called Gandhi!

*

Gandhiji had an unshakeable faith in the fundamental goodness of humanity. It was this latent fund of goodness in the human heart which he wanted to transmit.

Throughout his life, the affection and trust of those whose principles and policy he had to oppose had been a source of perennial satisfaction to Gandhiji.

With his boundless faith in human nature and in the redemptive power of truth, Gandhiji felt he must give everybody a chance to make good his bona fides.

He believed that if we trust our opponent, not out of fear, even when there is ground for distrust, the opponent will eventually reciprocate our trust. He had followed this principle throughout his life. A number of his opponents, including General Smut, became his friends due to this.

*

Gandhiji had to lead people to introspection and self-examination; to turn hardened hearts to genuine repentance; to steady friends and win over foes, even against what they mistook for their self-interest; to put heart into those who had been shaken by their sufferings and to bring love where hatred and cunning ruled.

Gandhiji touched the hearts of the millions in India because, by ceaseless striving, he had completely immersed his identity with those of millions, made their joys and sufferings his own, so much so that when they suffered, he suffered with them, when he suffered, they suffered too.

They clung to him. He had that magnetic pull. They might have been angry with him, they might even have quarrelled with him, but in their heart of hearts they knew that he was the friend of all; he loved them and theirs with a love greater than they themselves were, perhaps, capable of. They wanted him to guide them, even when they were not prepared to follow his advice.

With his dream of realizing unity in the land of his birth, a land threatened with destruction, Gandhiji became a radiating embodiment of contrasting forces, of hope and cheer, of quiet self-confidence and strength. There had been people visiting him in sorrow and in anger, in frustration and despair—some to mock, others to abuse. His unruffled equipoise and cool logic blunted the shafts of their anger. Those who came to quarrel stayed to adore, overwhelmed by his abundant love. Even when they were not convinced, they left their rancour behind and found a friend in him, whom they could not afford to lose. Those who came in depression and doubt went back cheerful and strong.

What was the secret of this baffling phenomenon? The answer is to be found in his utter self-effacement, his all-consuming longing to serve all living beings irrespective of any distinction. This was also the secret of his universal love which, transcending the transitory, enabled him to set his sights to the eternal.

*

Gandhiji's edifice of mass-satyagraha was built by the silent, selfless, unassuming workers—men, women and children who adopted the ashram lifestyle. This doesn't mean that they were trained in the ashram, but their belief in him is what constituted the Gandhi, the great leader. Outwardly, these workers had nothing much to show. They were mostly simple souls. They had their shortcomings and oddities. That some of them were endowed with a variety of versatile gifts is another matter. He made use of these. But it was not for these that he most valued them, but for their courage, faith and above all, their capacity to sacrifice themselves for the cause. They constituted

20

the stronghold, which he used time and again when his political colleagues hung back assailed by intellectual doubt. No wonder he did not stint giving his time and attention to discovering and moulding such workers and he gave them his best to get the best out of them. Gandhiji was the Master Builder.

*

People have often wondered what enabled Gandhiji to command and retain the devotion and sacrifice of so many diverse elements and hold them prisoners of his love. How did he manage to reconcile and harmonize such a vast medley of conflicting temperaments and interests to build up the power of non-violence? It was due to the reckless abandon with which he burned his candle at both ends to light the path of those who needed his guidance; the measure of his concern for and identification with those who had dedicated themselves to the cause; his mellowed wisdom; and the originality which he brought to bear upon whatever problem he touched.

*

Gandhiji literally believed in the dictum that one can serve the whole universe by doing one's allotted task steadfastly and well, and that it is better for one to die in the performance of one's own immediate duty than to be lured away by the prospect of the "distant scene", however attractive.

To Gandhiji, the test of a good worker was whether he knew how to match his work to the human material and the resources available at the moment and to fit his particular bit into the larger plan. A sound rule was to choose a few items that were within one's reach and capacity and work out the details while keeping the whole in view.

If the *satyagrahi* (practitioner of satyagraha) is not healthy in mind and body, he may fail in mustering complete fearlessness. He must not fall ill even if he has to bear cold, heat and rain; he will bear severe beatings, starvation and worse.

Samuel Butler, who in his *Erewhon* (a distopian novel of a land divested of machinery) put sick men in prison and criminals in hospitals, would have found in Gandhiji a kindred spirit. For, Gandhiji regarded sickness as a crime. He never excused it in himself or in others.

"I am unworthy to be your guide," he had told his co-detainees in the Aga Khan Palace after an attack of malaria had laid him low.

*

[On the 29th January, 1948] surveying the political scene, Gandhiji mused why Congressmen, who had toiled and sacrificed for the sake of freedom, and on whom now rested the burden of Independence, were succumbing to the lure of power? "Where will this take us?" And then, in a tone of infinite sadness he repeated the well-known verse of Nazir, the celebrated Urdu poet:

है बहारे बाग दुनिया चंद रोज
देख लो इसका तमाशा चंद रोज

(Short-lived is the splendour of spring in the garden of this world,
Watch the brave show while it lasts)

*

The funeral procession was about to start, when suddenly Sushila arrived from Lahore. On board the plane with her was Mian Iftekharuddin, a leader of West Punjab. He had rushed impulsively to Delhi to have Gandhiji's last *darshan* (vision or glimpse of the divine). As they alighted from the plane, he said to her in a choked voice: "My dear sister, the man who pulled the trigger is not Bapu's murderer. All of us who at any time doubted his word and entertained a feeling of communalism and violence in our hearts are responsible for his murder."

Pyarelal

[Compiled from *Mahatma Gandhi: The Last Phase*]

1

"DIRECT ACTION"

The Muslim League Council decided to launch "Direct Action" to achieve Pakistan. The 16th of August, 1946, was declared "Direct Action" Day, to be observed all over India as a day of protest. Immediately after the "Direct Action" resolution had been passed, Jinnah declared:

"Today we bid goodbye to constitutional methods." And further, "We have also forged a pistol and are in a position to use it."

"Direct Action," explained Liaquat Ali Khan, the right-hand man of Jinnah, meant "resorting to non-constitutional methods." He further added: "We cannot eliminate any method. 'Direct Action' means action against the law."

Abdur Rab Nishtar, League leader from the North-West Frontier, was reported to have said that Pakistan could only be achieved by shedding blood, and if the situation demanded, the blood of non-Muslims had to be shed.

There were communal disturbances and planned hooliganism in Ahmedabad, Bombay, Allahabad, Aligarh, Dacca and other places. Mysterious consignments of knives, daggers and other lethal weapons were intercepted by the police at various places all over India.

The Muslim League set up a Council of Action. It met behind closed doors, but the programme of action it drew up, and which was subsequently elaborated and broadcast by the Muslim League Press, was clear enough.

* * *

A Muslim League Government with Shaheed Suhrawardy as the Chief Minister was in power in Bengal.

Elaborate preparations for "Direct Action" were made in Calcutta for Direct Action in advance. As Minister in charge of Law and Order, Suhrawardy began systematically transferring out Hindu police officers from key posts. Thus on 16th August, 22 police stations out of 24 in Calcutta were in the charge of Muslim officers, and the remaining two were controlled by Anglo-Indians. August 16th was declared a public holiday by the Bengal Government, in spite of the warning and protests of the opposition in the Provincial Assembly. Many weapons including *lathis* (thick sticks), spears, hatchets, daggers and several other lethal weapons, including firearms, were distributed to the Muslims in large numbers and well in advance. Transport for League volunteers and hooligans was arranged. Rationing difficulties were overcome by issuing supplementary petrol coupons to the extent of several hundred gallons to the Ministers, just before the "Direct Action" Day.

From the midnight of 15th August, organized and armed bands of Muslims were seen moving about the streets rending the silence of the night with their militant cries and slogans. Muslim hooligans took to the business right from early morning on the 16th. By midday, the city came to a paralytic hault in many parts. The "Direct Action" Programme culminated in the Great Calcutta Killing on the 16th, 17th and 18th August. A huge procession of Muslims armed with *lathis*, spears and daggers started from Howrah for Calcutta, to attend a mass rally presided by Suhrawardy.

The conflagration became general towards evening and pandemonium prevailed all over the city when the rapidly increasing, unruly mobs returning from the grand rally began to interfere with those who did not join the *hartal* (strike). Their shops were looted, and the stock was thrown out into the streets. They started burning private cars and trams and stray pedestrians were assaulted and stabbed. The only vehicles seen on the streets were the Muslim League lorries and jeeps loaded with hooligans, shouting pro-Pakistan slogans and inciting the mob to violence.

Inferno was let loose on the city during the next two days, converting it into a vast shambles. Way ahead, in April 1946, Sir Feroz Khan

Noon, the ex-member of the Viceroy's Executive Council, had made an acid comment before the Muslim League Legislators' Convention that "the havoc which the Muslims would play would put to shame what Chengiz Khan did." While organized bands of hooligans, carrying Muslim League flags and shouting pro-Pakistan slogans, indulged in an unrestrained orgy of murder, arson, rape and looting, the police on the whole, especially for the first two days, stood passively by. The mob was elaborately armed for its destructive mission and the police was deliberately inactive. To make confusion worse, Suhrawardy established himself in the Control Room of the Police Headquarters, issuing verbal and written instructions, overriding decisions made by the police chief and generally interfering with their work. Towards evening, on the 16th August, Inspector Wade caught eight Muslims with a lorry-load of looted goods and sent them under arrest to the police station. Shortly after, Suhrawardy appeared there and ordered their immediate release on "his personal responsibility".

In some localities, the looting and killing went on for forty hours. The streets were strewn with dead bodies, and the foul odour of decaying corpses which lay unattended for days filled the air. Dead bodies had been pushed down the manholes, with the result that the drains were choked. Corpses lay in heaps in the bylanes, providing a gruesome feast to dogs, jackals and vultures; they were seen floating down the river; there were stories of children being hurled off the roofs of the houses or burnt alive; of women being raped, mutilated and then killed.

A fitter instrument could not have been found to put into effect the "Direct Action" Programme of the League than the efficient, intelligent and dynamic Bengal Chief Minister himself. Answering the charge of culpable failure to take adequate preventive measures in advance, he denied that the authorities had received any reports beforehand of "preparedness on the part of either the Hindus or the Muslims". The report of the Commissioner of Police on the Calcutta disturbances afterwards, however, clearly showed that the Intelligence Department *had received definite information*, among other things, that "goonda elements might cause disturbances if non-Muslims did not observe the *hartal*."

It was estimated that more than 5000 persons were killed and more than 15,000 injured during the Great Calcutta Killing. The military was called in on the third day, when the tide had already turned against those who had triggered off the conflagration. Giving his appreciation of the situation on the evening of the 17th August, when the military under him took charge of the city, Brigadier Sixsmith, the Area Commander, stated that "the police had not hitherto fired a single round. In one or two cases only tear-gas had been used."

Jinnah characterized it as an organized plot on the part of the Hindus to discredit the League Ministry of Bengal, and blamed it on the Congress and on Gandhiji!

2

THE STORM BURSTS

The "Direct Action" Programme of the Muslim League in Calcutta had misfired. It had recoiled on the heads of those who had launched it. So the cry went forth: "Calcutta must be avenged." Hell broke loose in Noakhali on the 10th October, 1946.

The principal crops of the Noakhali district are rice, jute, coconut and betel-nut. Due to the heavy rainfall, an intricate network of canals covers the whole district and provides a means of cheap transport for six months a year. The beautiful landscape spreads out the charm of the gardens. The tops of densely-growing coconut and betel-nut trees, rising to stately heights, almost meet overhead, forming a natural umbrella through which even the midday sun scarcely penetrates. Plantain and papaya, litchi and pineapple, luscious jackfruit and mango, and coconut with its cooling, refreshing milk—not to mention citrus—grow in abundance and are within almost everybody's reach. There is an endless variety of pot-herbs and vegetables, unrivalled in size and flavour, that can be grown with the minimum of labour; and about half a dozen varieties of roots and tubers growing practically in the wild. Ponds abound in fish and lotuses of many hues, while patches of bright heavens mirrored in the molten glass of the water-filled jute fields under the cloudless autumnal skies, present a vision of ravishing beauty which once seen can never be forgotten.

But behind this enchanting facade of nature lurks danger. The hamlets are widely scattered and isolated from one another by thick jungle growth, tall-growing jute fields and countless water channels.

A cry of distress even in the daytime is lost in the impenetrable solitude of the echoing woods that surround the hamlets, whilst the dense, interlacing vegetation and innumerable ponds and canals jammed with water hyacinth provide an ideal cover for the blackest of deeds.

On the 14th October, the following Press Note was released by the Bengal Press Advisory Committee:

> Reports of organized hooliganism in the district of Noakhali have reached Calcutta. Riotous mobs with deadly weapons are raiding villages, and looting, murder and arson are continuing since October 10 on a very large scale. Forcible mass conversion, abduction of women and desecration of places of worship are also reported.

According to another message, all ingress and egress of the persecuted people to and from the affected areas, were completely stopped and all approaches to these areas were closely guarded "by hooligans armed with deadly weapons".

According to Mr Taylor, Inspector-General of Police, the hooligans "were armed with guns and various types of other weapons and they were still defiant and not afraid to face the police and the military." As the mob proceeded, "they cut telegraph wires, demolished bridges, dammed canals and damaged and barricaded roads, making ingress and egress to and from the invaded localities impossible (or difficult)."

Admitting "very serious oppression" in Noakhali, the Chief Minister of Bengal stated that it had become somewhat difficult for the troops "to move in the affected areas as canals had been dammed, bridges damaged and roads blocked." The Chief Minister also stated that there had been forcible conversions, plunder and loot.

The first effect of the Noakhali outburst was stunning. It was followed by countrywide resentment and anger. What incensed public opinion even more than the slaughter and carnage was the evidence of offences against women, abduction, forced conversion, and forced marriages. The anger over these spread far beyond Bengal.

The refugees brought with them tales of gruesome happenings on a scale unprecedented in India's recent history. The houses of almost all well-to-do Hindu families had been burnt, systematic extortion of money under false assurances of protection had taken place, brutal assaults on hundreds of innocent people, forcible conversions of entire families, forcible marriages of unmarried and remarriage of married women to Muslims in the presence of their nearest and dearest ones had all happened. People who had been subjected to conversion and all sorts of tortures were forced to take forbidden food and perform Muslim religious rites.

Miss Muriel Lester, the English pacifist, happened to be in India at that time. On hearing about the Noakhali happenings, she straightway proceeded there. In a report from a relief centre in Noakhali she wrote:

> The worst of all was the plight of the women. Several of them had had to watch their husbands being murdered and then to be forcibly converted and married to some of those responsible for their death. These women had a dead look. It was not despair. It was utter blankness. The eating of beef and declaration of allegiance to Islam has been forced upon many thousands as the price of their lives. The goondas seem to think that they really are the rulers of this beautiful area of Bengal. One sees no sign of fear among those who had stood by and watched destruction, tyranny and aggression; anxiety as to future punishment does not seem to exist.

* * *

The failure of "Direct Action" in Calcutta was set down by its progenitors to the numerical inferiority of the Muslims compared to the other community. If the failure was to be retrieved, the blow had to be struck where the Muslims preponderated. Noakhali offered exceptional advantages.

The total area of the district was 1658 square miles. Out of 22 lakhs of the total population of Noakhali, 81 per cent were Muslims. Although Hindus constituted only 19 per cent of the population, they owned about 64 per cent of the *zamindary* (land possessed by a zamindar)—though the land was cultivated by tenants who were mostly Muslim. The Hindu landed gentry of Noakhali showed all the signs of a decadent aristocracy. They played a pivotal role and by their grit, enterprise, energy and organizing skill they cleared the jungle, built ponds, roads and canals, covered the countryside with plantations and developed the country in a variety of ways. But their later descendants fell easily to the abuses of inherited richness and gave themselves to the demoralizing effect of unearned income; they lost all those qualities and fell into a parasitic way of living. Moreover, they still adhered to the practices of untouchability though they were in minority.

The bulk of the Muslims of Noakhali were converts from Hinduism. As a class, they were simple, affable and peace loving, but illiterate and backward up to the limit of being timid. At the same time, they were extremely ignorant and easily ignitable, especially when their fanaticism was provoked. In such times they had the tendency to get together for any mass action.

It is not a widely known fact that Noakhali exports theologians and divines. In comparison to any other part of India, Noakhali has a larger number of maulanas and mullahs and it provides imams to most of the mosques in West Bengal and even to places as far away as Bombay and Madras (Chennai).

Quite a number of Noakhali Muslims were employed in Calcutta docks, factories and in various trades. A number of them returned to Noakhali after the Great Calcutta Killing and helped to spread tales of riot horrors which instigated the mass Muslim mind.

* * *

The holocaust commenced on the 10th October, the Lakshmi Puja Day. The rainy season was far advanced. The canals were overflowing with water. The rice fields were flooded. The District Board road was breached owing to heavy rains. Smaller roads were under water. The bamboo bridges were all guarded by the hooligans.

As the havoc spread from village to village, harrowing tales of fresh attacks on villages, massacres of entire families, mass conversion, arson and loot poured in.

The rioters arrived everywhere well prepared. Acting under leaders, they showed a high degree of organization. Nearly all their crimes were perpetrated in broad daylight. They attacked in great force, with a lightning suddenness, with inconceivable ruthlessness, especially when they encountered resistance. The slogans they were shouting: "*Allah-o-Akbar* (God is great)", "*Pakistan Zindabad* (long live Pakistan)", "*Larke Lenge Pakistan* (we shall take Pakistan by force)", *"Muslim League Zindabad* (long live the Muslim league)" and *"Kalikatar Pratishodh Chai* (we want revenge for Calcutta)". Their modus operandi involved a well-defined and uniform pattern; the actions were carried out in a planned hierarchy. First came extortion. Subscription was demanded in the name of the Muslim League. Assurance was held out that those who paid would be spared. The promise was not always kept. Even when life was spared, property was not.

After extortion, they would demand the surrender of all arms. The penalty for withholding a single weapon, even a scythe or a sickle, would mean instantaneous death to the whole family. Everything that could be removed was then plundered and the houses were set on fire with kerosene and petrol. It was locally reported that a month before these incidents took place, the ration shops had already stopped distributing kerosene in the affected areas.

After arson the mob would give in to looting. Everything that had escaped fire or was not completely burnt—door leaves, window frames, corrugated iron sheets etc—was looted. This went on for days together. The survivors were told that if they wanted to live they had to accept Islam. To prove their genuine conversion, the victims were supposed to give their unmarried, widowed and sometimes even married daughters in "marriage" to Muslims selected by the mob. In all these cases the village *maulvis* (learned Muslim scholars and teachers) became part of the mobs and were ready with their services, thus acting as hooligans and priests at the same time.

After conversion, guards were placed at the residence of the victims, ostensibly for their protection, but actually to prevent their escape and to make their conversion permanent. In some places, the ring-leaders had the temerity to issue "conversion" certificates as "safe conduct" passes to the families of victims going out of the cordoned areas.

* * *

Against this prevailing devastation, darkness and despair, there stood out instances of individual courage and heroism, fidelity and undying faith, reminding one that the divine spark in the human heart may be eclipsed but never extinguished. The law of non-violence is applicable even in the midst of carnage. At the same time, there were instances of Hindus who preferred death to conversion. There was the case of Navadwip Pandit of Raipur. At the invitation of the officer in charge, he had taken shelter in the police station at Raipur with a sum of Rs 20,000 in cash on his person. When the mob approached the *thana* (Police Station), the officer pushed him out. The mob relieved him of all his cash and demanded his conversion. He refused and chose to be killed with the name of God on his lips.

Even in this situation, there were incidents which proved to be a shine in the darkness, when a number of kind-hearted Muslims risked their lives to save their Hindu neighbours. In the village Hasnabad, Hindus and Muslims pledged themselves not to allow the peace of their locality to be affected. Learning that a batch of ruffians would meet at a particular place to formulate their plans of attack, the Muslims conveyed the information to the local police and all the ruffians were rounded up.

In yet another village, the life of a local Hindu doctor was saved by the solidarity of his Muslim neighbours who affirmed that they would kill anyone attacking the house of their doctor and posted guards to protect it. At Changirgaon, a band of looters came to a Hindu compounder's house and started looting and smashing religious pictures. A glass splinter from one of the picture frames entered into the foot of the leader of the band, causing profuse bleeding. The old practitioner thereupon, forgetting his own misfortune, took him to his half-ransacked dispensary and dressed his foot with all the care and attention he was capable of. The hooligans were taken aback by this unexpected return of good for evil. The chief ordered his men away and the house was saved from arson—the only house to escape in that locality.

* * *

The Noakhali tragedy, coming after the Great Calcutta Killing, made big headlines in the Press and gave a severe setback to the prestige of the Muslim League and particularly the League Government of Bengal.

As for the Government in office, they were only concerned with minimizing the seriousness of the happenings and maintaining before the world that nothing very serious had taken place.

The hooligans had been told by the gang leaders that whatever they did would be condoned, as it had the backing of the Government. It was, therefore, a shock to them when later, the police and the military arrived on the scene and gave an indication of taking energetic action. To get rid of them, an "atrocities" outcry was organized against them and even crimes against the modesty of Muslim women were invented. False cases were instituted against the police personnel as part of a general agitation for the withdrawal of the armed police and the military.

3

THE TRAVAIL

On a thin white mattress in his unfurnished whitewashed little room in the Bhangi Colony sat Gandhiji, discussing his future programme with Jawaharlal Nehru, in view of the Great Calcutta Killing and its aftermath. (The Bhangi Colony literally meant a colony of sweepers and toilet cleaners; the word "*bhangi*" is now no longer in use as it is considered offensive.) He was contemplating a return to Sevagram Ashram. Two days later came the news about Noakhali.

Gandhiji's friends felt perturbed. How would he be affected by this inferno, instigated with demoralization and despair on the one hand, and calculated falsehood and deceit on the other? He could have reacted to it by launching on a fast unto death. Wrote Miss Muriel Lester in a letter from Noakhali: The "well-planned Hitlerian network of folk" who organized the campaign would only be delighted at his death. She begged of Gandhiji not to launch on a fast, not only for the sake of his friends, but for the sake of the miscreants too, who needed his redeeming presence in their midst even more.

* * *

As Gandhiji sat listening to the stories pouring in from Noakhali, he resolved: "If I leave Delhi, it will not be in order to return to Sevagram, but only to go to Bengal. Else, I would stay here and stew in my juice."

Calcutta was still burning when Gandhiji left Delhi for Noakhali. The fire had never been completely put out since August, 1946.

"I do not know what I shall be able to do there," said Gandhiji. "All I know is that I won't be at peace with myself unless I go there."

Addressing the prayer meeting on the eve of his departure, Gandhiji remarked that it was a long and difficult journey he was setting out on and his health was poor. But one had to do one's duty and have undying trust in God. He requested people not to crowd at the stations on the way. India had given him enough affection. It needed no further demonstration. He was not going to Bengal to pass judgements on anybody; he was going there as a servant of God, hence he was to reach as the servant of all His creation.

There were mammoth crowds at all the big stations on the way. At places it was like a swarming ant-heap of humanity, as far as the eye could reach. The crowd clambered on to the roofs of the carriages, choked the windows, broke the glass, smashed the shutters and yelled and shouted till one's ears split. They pulled the alarm chain again and again for *darshan,* making it necessary to disconnect the vacuum brakes.

From Calcutta Station he was driven straight to Satish Chandra Das Gupta's Khadi Pratisthan Ashram at Sodepur. A gathering of several hundred had been waiting for him there for the evening prayer. He had reached Calcutta not with any set plan, but with a blank mind, to fulfill God's will.

Returning from a meeting with the Governor, as Gandhiji's car drove through the deserted streets with garbage heaps at places banked up nearly two feet high against the pavements, and rows of gutted shops and burnt-out houses in the side-streets and lanes extending as far as the eye could reach, he was overcome by a sinking feeling at the mass madness that could turn man into a brute. The only consolation was that such a state of things could not last. Human nature would not stand it.

A Muslim friend came and asked Gandhiji: "Why do you want to go to Noakhali? You did not go to Bombay, Ahmedabad or Chapra?" Was it because in other places it was the Muslims who were the sufferers, whereas in Noakhali they were Hindus? Would not his going to Noakhali under those circumstances add to the existing tension between Hindus and Muslims in India? Gandhiji replied that he would certainly have gone to any of the places mentioned by the friend, if anything approaching what had happened in Noakhali had happened there and if he felt that he could do nothing for those places without being on the spot. He had decided not to leave Bengal until the last embers of the trouble were stamped out. "I may stay on here for a whole year or more. If necessary, I will die here. But I will not acquiesce in failure. If the only effect of my presence in the flesh is to make people look up to me in hope and expectation which I can do nothing to vindicate, it would be far better that my eyes were closed in death."

This was the first indication he gave to the public of the "Do or Die" resolve that was shaping in his mind.

* * *

Yet, with all his impatience to reach Noakhali as quickly as possible, four more days elapsed before Gandhiji could actually leave Calcutta. They turned out to be the most fruitful period of his mission.

The Muslim festival of Baqr-Id, when, in commemoration of the sacrifice of Abraham, the Muslims sacrifice cows, was close at hand and the possibility of a communal clash could not be dismissed. The Chief Minister of Bengal suggested that Gandhiji should extend his stay in Calcutta to consolidate the peace in the city at least till Baqr-Id was over. What was the use of proceeding to Noakhali while Calcutta was burning?

There were people who distrusted the bona fides of the Chief Minister, whom they held responsible for the Great Calcutta Killing and other misdeeds too numerous to mention. They suggested to Gandhiji that the Chief Minister's request was only a trick to delay his going to Noakhali if it could not be prevented altogether; that on the Baqr-Id day the riot-victims in Noakhali, who had been forcibly converted to Islam and were now marooned, might be made to slaughter cows and eat beef and so on. But all these arguments did not impress Gandhiji. To him, they smacked of fear and distrust. Non-violence knew neither. He would trust the Chief Minister and take his proposal at face value. He could not begin by distrusting the person whom he was out to convert by his love.

If he extended his stay in Calcutta at the request of Shaheed Suhrawardy to consolidate the peace in the city, he reasoned, it would mean that the onus of maintaining the peace of Noakhali during that interval would rest upon Shaheed. Shaheed had given his solemn assurance on that score. It would be a matter of his honour. But supposing Shaheed failed to keep his promise, said Gandhiji, he would take that risk. It was an article of faith with him that if we trust our opponent, even when there is ground for distrust, and not out of fear, the opponent will end up reciprocating. This also demands that we act consistently on the square to the last. He had followed that principle throughout his life.

Gandhiji had known the Bengal Chief Minister from the good old Khilafat days. Shaheed, at that time, used to take pride in calling himself Gandhiji's "son". If only he could have re-awakened that chord in him! He decided to begin his mission in Noakhali by trying to conquer the person who, in the popular belief, was responsible for the Noakhali trouble.

"How is it, Shaheed Saheb, that everybody calls you the chief of the goondas? Nobody seems to have a good word to say about you!" Gandhiji began his first meeting with his would-be collaborator.

"Mahatmaji, don't people say things about you, too, behind your back?" replied Shaheed nonchalantly.

"That may be," replied Gandhiji laughing. "Still, there are at least some who call me Mahatma. But I have not heard a single person calling you a Mahatma!"

Without turning a hair, Shaheed replied: "Mahatmaji, don't believe what people say about you in your presence!"

Gandhiji's jokes were never without a purpose. He could not expect to convert Shaheed if he hid from him what people were saying about him. Absolute frankness was the precondition for mutual trust. It broke the ice completely between them and enabled them to shed their inhibitions. Thereafter, Shaheed knew that he could love the man who knew him to the core and had the courage to tell him what he knew, without being detracted from the affection he bore towards him.

In the succeeding days, they hammered out a formula for the establishment of communal harmony in Bengal. Fundamentals of far-reaching importance were embodied in their joint declaration: "It is our certain conviction that Pakistan cannot be brought about by communal strife, nor can India be kept whole through the same means. It is also our conviction that there can be no conversion or marriage by force; nor has abduction any place in a society which has any claim to be called civilized."

It further embodied the vital principle that religion could not sanctify any breach of fundamental morality.

* * *

Before Gandhiji could proceed to Noakhali, Bihar put him to the test. The news about the happenings in Calcutta and Noakhali had travelled fast and set up a widespread ferment in the neighbouring province of Bihar, converting it into a vast powder-magazine. The cry for reprisals had already gone forth. Gandhiji was shocked to hear that some Muslims, while fleeing from Bihar in panic, had been set on fire and killed by Hindus.

On the 3rd November, *Morning News,* a Muslim League paper from Calcutta, came out with news about extensive rioting in Bihar. Immediately, Gandhiji wired Jawaharlal Nehru who, with three of his colleagues in the Interim Government—Sardar Patel, Liaquat Ali Khan and Abdur Rab Nishtar—had proceeded to Patna, asking for details. Nehru wired back informing him that the situation was tense in many parts, but the Government was doing their best to bring it under control; he further mentioned that, along with Abdur Rab Nishtar, he had decided to stay back in Bihar as long as it was necessary.

Revenge was neither the way of peace nor of humanity, Gandhiji observed in his prayer address. If they could not be generous enough to forgive a person who gave them a slap, they could give one in return. But supposing the actual perpetrator of the crime ran away and the injured party slapped his relation or his co-religionist by way of retaliation, it would be below human dignity. "If someone abducts my daughter, am I to abduct his or his friends daughter? The cry of blood for blood is barbarous. You cannot take revenge in Bihar for the happenings in Noakhali."

There were many frequent telephonic calls between the Sodepur Ashram and Patna that night. "Mahatmaji alone can save us," phoned a Muslim League leader of Bihar, Mohammad Yunus. "Should he start immediately?" I asked. "He is ready." "No," he replied, "there is no immediate need. He can take his time. For now, the presence of Pandit Nehru and other Cabinet Ministers is enough."

"Pretty bad," was Jawaharlal Nehru's reply to a telephone inquiry on behalf of Gandhiji. "But we are rapidly regaining control." "Any crimes against women?" I asked. "They are not absent."

It was enough to fill Gandhiji's cup of anguish to the brink. "If Congressmen fail to protect Muslims where the Congress is in power, then what is the use of having a Congress Government?" he commented in a written message to the prayer gathering the next day. "Similarly, if the League Premier could not afford protection to the Hindus, what business had he to be there? And if either of them had to take the aid of the military in order to protect the Muslim or the Hindu minority in their respective provinces, it only meant that none of them actually exercised any control over the general population in a crisis. This is a matter over which all of us should ponder deeply." He deprecated the smug habit of exonerating themselves by blaming it all on the goondas. "We always put the blame on the goondas. But it is we who make the goondas and encourage them. It is not right to say that all the wrong that has been done is the work of the goondas."

He repeated the warning even more forcefully on the 5th November. The Hindus could have said: "Did not the Muslims start the trouble?" He wanted them not to succumb to the temptation to retort in that way, but to turn the searchlight inward and think of their own duty irrespective of what the other party did. There was a moral code even for the use of violence. If they gave way to the impulse of revenge and retaliation, the flames of violence would consume those who lit them. Independence would vanish into thin air and a third power, "be it the British or any other", would be firmly planted in India if they continued quarrelling with each other. He did not care if they were all destroyed. But he could not countenance the destruction of India's freedom.

Everybody heaved a sigh of relief when Baqr-Id passed off quietly all over India. But the news from Bihar had set Gandhiji at war with himself. "Principally for reasons of health, soon after coming to Calcutta, I had gone on a spare, milkless diet," he wrote in a letter to Rajkumari Amrit Kaur. "Subsequent happenings in the country induced me to prolong it. Now Bihar will send me to complete fast if things do not radically mend. There will be no time limit." On the following day, he wrote to Jawaharlal Nehru:

The news from Bihar has shaken me. My own duty seems to me clear. Although I have striven hard to avert a fast, I can do so no longer. My inner voice tells me, "You may not live to be a witness to this senseless slaughter. If people refuse to see what is clear as daylight and pay no heed to what you say, does it not mean that your day is over?" The logic of the argument is driving me irresistibly towards a fast. I, therefore, propose to issue a statement that unless this orgy of madness ceases, I must go on a fast unto death. You can strive with me, if you think differently. But knowing as you do my temperament, I am sure you will approve of my proposed step. In any event, you will go on with your work without a moment's thought about my possible death and leave me in God's good care. No worry allowed.

But neither Jawaharlal Nehru nor Sardar Patel tried to dissuade him. They understood better the magnitude of the stake. It was nothing less than India's independence. Before leaving for Noakhali on the 6th November, Gandhiji issued an appeal entitled *To Bihar*:

The Bihar of my dreams seems to have falsified them. It is easy enough to retort that things under the Muslim League Government in Bengal were no better, if not worse, and that Bihar is merely a result of the latter. A bad act of one party is no justification for a similar act by the opposing party. Is counter-communalism any answer to the communalism of which Congressmen have accused the Muslim League? Is it nationalism to seek barbarously to crush the fourteen per cent of the Muslims in Bihar?

I do not need to be told that I must not condemn the whole of Bihar for the sake of the sins of a few thousand Biharis. I am afraid, if the misconduct in Bihar continues, all the Hindus of India will be condemned by the world. That is its way, and it is not a bad way either. Let not Bihar, which has done so much to raise the prestige of the Congress, be the first to dig its grave.

I do not want in this letter to talk of Ahimsa to you. I do want, however, to tell you that what you are reported to have done is worse than cowardice. It is unworthy of nationalism or any religion. What you have done is to degrade yourselves and drag down India.

You should tell Pandit Jawaharlalji, Nishtar Saheb and Dr Rajendra Prasad to take away their military and themselves and attend to the affairs of India. This they can only do if you repent your inhumanity and assure them that Muslims are as much your care as your own brothers and sisters. You should not rest till every Muslim refugee has come back to his home which you should undertake to rebuild.

I regard myself as a part of you. Your affection has compelled that loyalty in me. And since I claim to have better appreciation than you seem to have of what Bihari Hindus should do, I cannot rest till I have done some measure of penance.

After setting down the terms of his proposed fast unless the madness in Bihar ceased and the erring Biharis turned over a new leaf, the statement proceeded: "What my penance should do is to quicken the conscience of those who know me and believe in my bona fides."

Fasting is the most powerful weapon in the armoury of satyagraha, but extremely dangerous on that very account if wrongly used. There are definite rules governing its use. It is not fasting by itself that matters, but what lies behind the fast, that is, self-purification. If it is of sufficient intensity, it must result in an all-round purification of society, including the opponent.

Gandhiji's decision to launch on to a partial fast, and on to a total one if things did not mend immediately in Bihar, had an electrical effect on the Bihar situation.

* * *

Accompanied by Shamsuddin Ahmed, the Minister of Labour, and two Parliamentary Secretaries of the Bengal Government—Nasrullah Khan and Abdur Rashid—Gandhiji set out from Sodepur on the 6th November, by the special train which the Chief Minister had arranged.

At Goalando, the river journey began. Travelling down the Padma nearly 100 miles by steamer, Gandhiji and party reached Chandpur late at night. The night was passed on the steamer in mid-stream.

The next morning, before Gandhiji entrained for Chaumuhani —his destination in Noakhali—two deputations waited on board the *SS Kiwi*: one Muslim, the other Hindu. The former deputation consisted of several prominent Muslim Leaguers. They seemed to be in a resentful and acrimonious mood. One of them remarked that no disturbances had taken place in the Chandpur subdivision; the rush of refugees to Chandpur was due to panic caused by "false Press propaganda"; the number of Hindus killed by the Muslims was only 15, while double that number of Muslims had died as a result of firing by the military, who were mostly Hindus. Another member of the deputation was bitter over the fact that the Hindus were still fleeing and their rehabilitation was being "obstructed" by Hindu workers who encouraged them to migrate in order to discredit the Muslim League Government and paralyze the administration!

Shamsuddin Ahmed, the Minister accompanying Gandhiji, interposed. It was no use isolating the Chandpur subdivision and ignoring what had taken place elsewhere in the district. Equally irrelevant was their reference to the military firing. At last, it was Gandhiji's turn to speak. He began: If what they had said was to be taken at its face value, then it amounted to this—that the Muslims were innocent; the mischief had all been provoked by false propaganda and excesses by the police and the military, who, therefore, with the panic-mongering Hindus were the real culprits! That was too big a pill for anybody to swallow. Why had it become necessary to call in the military if no disturbances had taken place? Even Muslim Leaguers had admitted that terrible things had happened; they only disputed the figures. He was not concerned with the numbers. Even if a single case of abduction, forcible conversion or forcible marriage had taken place, it was enough to make every God-fearing man hang down his head in shame. The right course was to make a clean breast of the matter. "It is far better to magnify your mistake and proclaim it to the whole world than leave it to the world to point the accusing finger at you. God never spares the evildoer." He had come to promote mutual goodwill and confidence, he proceeded. For this he needed their help. He did not want peace to be established with the help of the police and the military, nor did he wish to encourage people to flee from their homes.

Still another member of the deputation said that only one per cent of the people had indulged in acts of hooliganism; the rest—99 per cent—were really good people and in no way responsible for the happenings.

Gandhiji disapproved of this way of thinking. He said that if the 99 per cent who were "good people" had actively disapproved of what had taken place, the one per cent would have been able to do nothing and could have easily been brought to books. "Good people ought to actively combat the evil to entitle them to that name. Sitting on the fence is no good." His respect for the Prophet of Islam was not less than theirs. But authoritarianism and compulsion were the way to corrupt a religion, not to advance it.

Shamsuddin Ahmed, agreeing with Gandhiji, quoted a verse from the Koran to the effect that there can be no compulsion in religion. He had told the Muslims, he said, that if they wanted Pakistan they must mete out justice to the minority community and win its confidence. By doing what they had done, they had killed Pakistan.

Gandhiji was shown an official notice, issued by Mr McInerny, the District Magistrate of Noakhali, to the effect that unless the contrary was conclusively proved, he would assume "that anyone who accepted Islam after the beginning of the recent disturbances was forcibly converted and in fact remained a Hindu." Referring to it, Gandhiji said that if all the Muslims endorsed that declaration, it would go a long way to settle the question. It was up to the leaders of the Muslims to declare that forcible repetition of a formula did not make a non-Muslim into a Muslim.

One of them, thereupon, remarked that on their part they were all prepared to go into the interior along with the Hindu leaders to restore peace, but the latter were not prepared to trust them. Gandhiji said that it did not matter. "You and I shall visit every village and every home in the interior and restore peace and confidence."

The members of the deputation had come with their minds full of prejudice. They had expected to be met by a hail of fire and brimstone. They were surprised to find that, while Gandhiji did not hesitate to point out to them where the Muslims had erred, he had not one angry word against the Muslims as such. He had even expressed himself against the employment of the military and the police and against the mass migration of the Hindus. Surely, this man could not be their enemy.

The other deputation consisted of a group of about 20 Hindu workers. Some of them were prominent Congressmen of the district. The group included several representatives of various relief organizations as well. "If you say you cannot do without police or military protection," Gandhiji said to them, "you really confess defeat even before the battle has begun. No police or military in the world can protect people who are cowards. What goes against the grain in me is that a single individual can be forcibly converted or a single woman kidnapped or molested. So long as you feel you *can* be subjected to these indignities, you *shall* continue to be so subjected. Your trouble is not numerical inferiority but the feeling of helplessness that has seized you and the habit of depending on others. That is why I am opposed to the idea of your migrating from East Bengal en masse. It is no cure for impotence or helplessness."

The members of the deputation demanded that Muslim police and Muslim military in the area should be replaced by Hindu cadres in order to restore confidence amongst the Hindus. Gandhiji told them it was a false cry. The Hindu police and Hindu military had in the past done against their Hindu brethren all the things that they had complained of. "I come from Kathiawad—the land of petty principalities. No woman's honour is safe in some of these principalities.

"No, I am not going to leave you in peace. Presently, you will ask yourselves: 'When will this old man leave us and go?' But this old man will *not* go. He did not come on your invitation and he will go only on his own, but with your blessings, when his mission in East Bengal is fulfilled."

"Here we are a mere drop in the ocean," remarked another friend, resuming the discussion.

Gandhiji replied that even if there was only one Hindu in East Bengal, he wanted that Hindu to have the courage to go and live in the midst of the Muslims and die, if he must, like a hero. He would then command even the admiration of the Muslims. "There is not a man, however cruel and hard-hearted, but would give his admiration to a brave man. A goonda is not as much a vile man as he is imagined to be. He is not without his redeeming features."

The company included a number of young men who had been members of a terrorist group that had successfully organized in the past the famous raid on the Chittagong Armoury, with a daring and courage that had extorted the admiration even of the British officials. The friend who was leading the argument had been a member of that group. He was still unconvinced: "A goonda does not understand reason. But he understands bravery. If he finds that you are braver than he, he will respect you."

"You will note," Gandhiji continued, "that for the purpose of our present discussion I have not asked you to discard the use of arms. The most tragic thing about the armoury raid people is that their bravery did not infect others."

"I am an armoury raid man myself."

"You are no armoury raid man, or you would not have lived to tell me these things. That so many of you should have remained alive, witnesses to the things that have happened here is, in my eyes, a tragedy of the first magnitude. If you had shown the same fearlessness and courage to face death in the present crisis as at the time of that raid, you would have gone down in history as heroes. As it is, you have only inscribed a small footnote in the page of history. You will see I am not asking you merely to follow my type of heroism. I have not made it good a hundred per cent even in my own case. I have come here to test it out in East Bengal. I want you to take to the conventional type of heroism. You should be able to infect others, both men and women, with the courage and fearlessness that are needed to face death when the alternative is dishonour and humiliation. Thus only can the Hindus stay in East Bengal, not otherwise."

"The proportion of Muslims and Hindus here is six to one. How can you expect us to face such heavy odds?"

"When India was brought under British subjection, there were only 70,000 European soldiers against 33 crores of Indians."

"We have no arms. The hooligans have the backing of Government bayonets."

That gave Gandhiji the opportunity to describe to them the superiority of satyagraha (soul-force) over conventional weapons in the face of overwhelming odds. The Indian community in South Africa was a mere handful in the midst of an overwhelming majority of Europeans and natives. "The Europeans had arms. We had none. So we forged the weapon of Satyagraha. Today, the Indian is respected by the white man in South Africa, not so the Zulu, with all his fine physique."

"So, we are to fight with arms anyhow?" the ex-terrorist friend finally remarked.

"Not anyhow," Gandhiji replied. "Even violence has its code of ethics. For instance, to butcher helpless old men, women and children is not bravery but rank cowardice. Chivalry requires that they should be protected even at the cost of one's life. The history of early Islam is replete with such instances of chivalry and Islam is all the stronger for it."

"Use your arms well, if you must," he concluded. "Do not ill use them. Bihar has not used its arms well. It is the privilege of arms to protect the weak and the helpless. The best help that Bihar could have given to the Hindus of East Bengal would have been to guarantee with their own lives the absolute safety of the Muslim population living in their midst. Their example would then have told. And I have faith that they will still do so with due repentance—when the present madness has passed away. At any rate, that is the price I have put upon my life, if they want me to live. Here ends the first lesson."

4

A VENTURE IN FAITH

Laksham was the next big halt, where there was a big refugee camp. And it was to the refugees assembled at the railway station that Gandhiji's words were addressed. He had vowed, he declared, not to leave Bengal until peace was restored and even a solitary Hindu girl was not afraid to move about freely in the midst of the Muslims. The greatest help they could give him was to banish fear from their hearts. "Why should you be afraid of the cry of *Allah-o-Akbar*? The Allah of Islam is the same as the Rama of the Hindus— the protector of the innocent. To run away from danger instead of facing it is to deny one's faith in God."

The party reached Chaumuhani. Volunteers under Charu Chowdhury, a seasoned *satyagrahi*, had reached there a week in advance to make arrangements for Gandhiji's arrival. It was all chaos and confusion everywhere when they arrived. The town itself had remained free from disturbance, but the surroundings had been set ablaze. There was consternation, anger and demoralization among all sections. The place stank after the recent rains. No one was ready to put in labour, for love or money. Everyone was too scared to help.

People met, discussed and argued excitedly and dispersed without advancing an inch. The intelligentsia were highly demoralized. Many of them directly blamed the non-violence propounded by Gandhiji!

Patiently, Charu and his volunteers set to work with the technique of constructive work taught by Gandhiji. The workers issued forth with baskets, brooms and spades, converting themselves into scavengers and day-labourers. A road had to be repaired, a prayer ground to be marked out and levelled, sanitary arrangements to be made. It was a slow and uphill task. But they persevered. As their work progressed, difficulties were overcome one after another. Even those who were initially sceptical got motivated. The spectre of apathy and despair began to dissolve. Some even offered to assist. Even the Muslims began to take interest in and appreciate what the workers were doing against heavy odds. By the time Gandhiji arrived, not only was the road built, the prayer ground ready and the sanitary arrangements in perfect condition, but all this had built up the morale of the affected people in the area and introduced a whiff of life-giving fresh air into the choking atmosphere of the place. Slowly, order began to emerge from the welter of confusion.

The Bengal Government had adopted elaborate security measures for Gandhiji's protection during his Noakhali stay. The arrival of the armed police and the military with a fleet of jeeps, armoured-cars and trucks created consternation among the local Muslims. The bazaar buzzed with rumours. One of them was that Gandhiji had come with a contingent of goondas—an expression applied in Noakhali to anyone they did not like! Several prominent local Muslim Leaguers met Gandhiji on his arrival at Chaumuhani. They were agreeably surprised when Gandhiji told them that he was no more enamoured of the police and the military than they were.

"How can we create a sense of security and self-confidence in the present state of things?" asked a Hindu young man who met Gandhiji.

"By learning to die bravely. Forget the military and the police. They are broken reeds."

A woman worker came to Gandhiji. She was an ex-terrorist. She felt very depressed by the plight of the women. She asked him, "What is your idea of rehabilitation?"

"Not to send them to Assam and West Bengal but to infuse courage into them so that they are not afraid to stay in their own homes."

"How is that possible?"

"You must stay in their midst and tell them that you are not going to leave them till the last of them is safe. Then you will produce heroines in East Bengal."

"That was once our idea too," rejoined the woman worker.

"I do not mind if each and every one of the 500 families in your area is done to death," continued Gandhiji. "Here, you are 20 per cent of the population. In Bihar, the Muslims constitute only 14 per cent."

"They know they won't be molested there."

"They have been butchered in a more brutal manner and there have been cases of molestation of women, too, this time."

"If the Government do not provide rations?"

"Rations can be purchased, but honour and self-respect cannot be bought."

The woman worker, shedding her initial scepticism exclaimed: "You have opened up a new vista before us, Mahatmaji. We feel fresh blood coursing through our veins."

Chaumuhani had a population of not more than 5000. But on the day of Gandhiji's arrival, there was a crowd of not less than 15,000 at the evening prayer meeting, large numbers having come from the surrounding areas. About 80 per cent of them were Muslims. Addressing them, Gandhiji said that he had come to speak to them not in anger but in grief. Ever since he had come to Bengal, he had been hearing awful tales of Muslim atrocities. Shaheed Suhrawardy, all the Ministers of the Bengal Government and the League leaders who had met him in Calcutta had condemned them unequivocally. "They are a blot on the name of Islam. I have studied the Koran. The very word 'Islam' means peace. The Muslim greeting *Salaam Alaikum* (peace be upon you) is the same for all—whether Hindus, Muslims, or any other. Nowhere does Islam permit such things as have happened in Noakhali. The Muslims are in such an overwhelming majority in East Bengal that it is up to them to constitute themselves into the guardians of the small Hindu minority and to tell Hindu women that while they are there, no one dare cast an evil eye on them."

Shamsuddin Ahmed, the League Minister, followed it up the next day with a warning that the issue of Pakistan versus Hindustan was not going to be settled by the slaughter of Hindus where Muslims were in a majority and vice versa. No Government worth its name could stand silently by and let the majority oppress or exterminate the minority. All that had happened, including forcible conversions and the like, was un-Islamic. It was for the Muslims of Noakhali to reassure the Hindus and set them at ease. The miscreants had to be punished for their crimes and it was the duty of the Muslims in general to help the authorities to trace them and bring them to book. He hoped that out of the ashes of the conflagration, the edifice of abiding Hindu-Muslim unity would be rebuilt in Bengal.

* * *

Emerald-green fields of paddy met the eye everywhere on the way as, accompanied by the two Parliamentary Secretaries, the District Magistrate and the Superintendent of Police, Gandhiji set out from Chaumuhani to penetrate into the interior. There had been a bumper crop such as the district had not known for 12 years. But nature's bounty was more than offset by the sadistic cruelty of man. The grain was in the earth and about to ripen, but the bulk of those who had sown were not there to reap. Some had been killed, others had fled for safety to various refugee camps. Unless the displaced returned to their homes quickly, the standing paddy and betel-nut crops would be lost or stolen in the absence of the owners.

Addressing a gathering of over 10,000 Hindus and Muslims in the evening at Dattapara, Gandhiji observed that it was a shame for both the Hindus and the Muslims that the Hindus should have had to run away from their homes. He knew the Hindus had suffered a lot and were suffering still. But it served no useful purpose to keep on recalling the past. They were to forgive and forget and, if the necessary guarantee was forthcoming, they were to return to their homes with courage.

A Hindu refugee got up and asked how they could have confidence in the assurance of the Muslims any more. When the threat was impending, they had promised to look after them, but had failed to protect them afterwards. Besides, there were no homes to return to; they had lost everything. Were they to go back and live in the ruins? Gandhiji remarked that the Government had promised that their huts would be rebuilt and they would be provided food and clothing when they returned. Whatever might have happened in the past, if one good Muslim and one good Hindu took the responsibility for their safety in each village, they could rely on their word, as it would be followed by the collective assurance of goodwill of all the Muslims in the village. If they were still afraid, then they were cowards and even God could not help the coward.

* * *

Gandhiji asked the Muslims to search their hearts and tell whether they really wanted the Hindus to come back and live in their midst as friends and neighbours.

"Whether you believe me or not, I want to assure you that I am a servant of both the Hindus and the Muslims. I have not come here to fight Pakistan. If India is destined to be partitioned, I cannot prevent it. But I ask my Muslim brethren to search their hearts and if they do not wish to live as friends with the Hindus, to say so openly. The Hindus must, in that case, leave East Bengal and go somewhere else. The refugees cannot stay on as refugees forever. The Government cannot go on feeding them for an indefinite period. Nor can they subsist for long, as they are subsisting at present, on less than half the daily ration of cereals to keep an able-bodied man alive; no fish, no vegetables, nor anything else to supplement it with. But even if each Hindu leaves, I shall still continue to live amidst the Muslims of East Bengal. I will not avail of any food from outside, but subsist on what they give me and what I consider lawful for me to partake of. If, on the other hand, you want the Hindus to stay in your midst, you should tell them that they need not look to the military for protection, but to their Muslim brethren instead. Their daughters and sisters and mothers are your daughters, sisters and mothers, and you should protect them with your lives. You should ponder what I have said and let me know what you really wish. I shall advise the Hindus accordingly."

He was physically exhausted after a week's semi-fast. The daily nourishment counted less than 600 calories. To conserve strength, he had to consent to being carried to the prayer ground in an improvised chair slung over a pole and borne on the shoulders by some members of his party. His voice was feeble and the face bore marks of deep anguish. But there was not a trace of anger or impatience in the speech. It breathed only forgiveness and love. In fact, he told the bluntest truth, kept back nothing, nor suppressed anything. Yet it did not hurt. The people felt as if it was their better self speaking to them. The anguished voice of love they heard excluded nobody. It was a strong, passionate appeal to their conscience. What came from the heart went straight to the heart.

The discussion was resumed in a conference with the District Magistrate and some officials. There were, besides, representatives of the refugees and the local Muslims. It was explained by a *maulvi* that the Muslims, far from wanting to drive away the Hindus, felt insecure themselves, as a number of them with status and standing had been put under arrest although they were innocent and that was the real obstacle in the way of their befriending the Hindus.

Gandhiji replied that, "It is obvious that when large numbers have participated in crime, some innocent men will be implicated with the guilty ones. It is so all over the world. That does not mean that the guilty ones should not be proceeded against." The remedy was for the Muslims to confer with the Hindus and produce agreed lists of those who had actually been guilty. No innocent person would then suffer. For the authorities, as well as for Muslims, it was an acid test to bring to books the guilty.

Addressing the members of the Muslim League in the gathering, Gandhiji proceeded: "I have come here to seek your cooperation. You are a powerful party. The first question we have got to settle is whether there *can* be cooperation between the Hindus and the Muslims."

It was a vital issue. If the Hindus could live side by side with the Muslims in Noakhali, the two communities could coexist in the rest of India, too, without the vivisection of the Motherland. Thus the fate of India hung upon Noakhalis reaction to the challenge.

* * *

Gandhiji shifted from Dattapara to Kazirkhil—right in the heart of the devastation.

At Kazirkhil, Gandhijis camp was set up in the partially devastated house of a prosperous Hindu of the locality. No one was staying there at that time. An advance party of volunteers had cleaned it up and made it worth living in. In the course of his post-prayer addresses,

Gandhiji observed that he found indescribable peace in the natural scenery around him, but he found that peace missing on the faces of men and women. There were no tears in his eyes, he said. He who shed tears could not wipe those of others. But his heart was wailing. He had carried on a grim struggle against the Government for 20 years in South Africa and for the last 30 years in India. But the fratricide that they were facing was more awful than anything else within his experience. He had resolved not to leave Bengal empty-handed. The word "pessimism" was not to be found in his dictionary. The Muslims had butchered the Hindus and did worse things than butchery in Bengal, and the Hindus had butchered the Muslims in Bihar. When both acted wickedly it was no use making comparisons or saying which one was less wicked than the other, or who started the trouble. If they wished to take revenge, they should learn the art from him. He, too, took revenge, but it was of a different type. He had read a Gujarati poem in his childhood which said: "If to him who gives you a glass of water you give two, there is no merit in it. Real merit lies in doing good to him who does you evil." That was his conception of noble revenge.

Four miles south-east of Kazirkhil was the village Dasgharia. Amtus Salam, a devout Muslim woman inmate of Gandhiji's Ashram had preceded Gandhiji there. Practically all the Hindu women in the village who had been converted to Islam during the disturbances had returned to their original faith. On the occasion of Gandhiji's visit, they all came out in one spirit and greeted him by mass singing of *Ramadhun* (Rama's name sung repeatedly as a part of prayer). Thanks to Gandhiji's peace mission, before long there was not one forcibly converted person left throughout Noakhali who had not reverted to his or her original faith.

In a written message that was read out at a prayer gathering, Gandhiji described the anatomy of fear. "The more I go about in these parts, the more I find that your worst enemy is fear. The terrorist as well as the terrorized are equally its victims. It eats into their vitals. Unless you cultivate fearlessness, there will never be any peace in these parts for the Hindus or for the Muslims."

At the request of the women from the village of Madhupur, Gandhiji held a women's meeting the next day. He was told that there were some women in the villages who wanted to come away but wanted military escort. Gandhiji told them he could never be party to such a request. Hindus and Muslims should be free to break each others heads if they wanted to. It was up to the men to tell the women that they would be their escort and would protect them with their lives. If still the women were afraid to come, there was no help for them. Those who preferred security to freedom had no right to live. He had come to proclaim from the housetops that women had to become brave or else perish. They should make use of the calamity that had befallen them to cast out the demon of fear.

* * *

While Gandhiji, in spite of his semi-fast, was thus wearing out in a ceaseless endeavour to reach the hearts of the officials, the Muslim Leaguers, the riot victims and the local Muslims alike, a resolution was slowly forming in his mind.

The criminal elements had been threatening the Hindus that the Mahatma was not going to be in their midst forever. The Hindus, on the other hand, were perturbed to find that instead of supporting their demand for more police and more military protection, he deprecated both. Once the police and military are withdrawn, they would again be marooned and left to the tender mercies of their erstwhile oppressors. The prospect froze them with horror. The dry season was fast approaching. The canals would soon dry up and deprive them of the one means of easy transport. Their only chance of safety lay in making good their escape before the mouse-trap closed upon them once more. An answer had to be found to their fears.

Gandhiji could not sit still. He had to act. He had come to the decision that he would break up his camp, deprive himself of the services of all his companions and bury himself in East Bengal until a time came when the Hindus and the Muslims learnt to live together in harmony and peace. He would fend for himself with whatever local assistance he was able to command. All the members of his party, including the women, would settle down, each in one affected village, and make themselves hostages for the safety and security of the Hindus in that village. He didn't force anyone to follow him. He said, "Those who have ill will against the Muslims or disrespect for Islam in their hearts or cannot curb their indignation at what has happened should stay away." So far as he was concerned, he announced, his decision was final and irrevocable.

A discussion with the members of his party followed. His ahimsa would be incomplete, Gandhiji explained, unless he took that step. "I know the women of Bengal better than, probably, the Bengalis do. Today they feel crushed and helpless. The sacrifice of myself and my companions would at least teach them the art of dying with self-respect. It might open the eyes of the oppressor too, and melt their hearts. I do not say that the moment my eyes are closed theirs will open. But that it will be the ultimate result, I have not the shadow of a doubt. If ahimsa disappears, Hindu religion disappears."

"How can you reason with people who are thirsting for your blood? Only the other day two of our workers were murdered," interposed another of the company.

"I know it. But to quell the rage is our job."

In a letter to a friend he wrote: "The work I am engaged in here may be my last act. If I return from here alive and unscathed, it will be like a new birth. My ahimsa is being tried here through and through as it never was before."

* * *

Two days later, Gandhiji took another important step forward. He would live in a Muslim household if a Muslim Leaguer approved of by the Bengal Ministry would be prepared to receive him as a member of the family.

He was in the midst of a Muslim population in Noakhali. He would not, therefore, like to stay in a Hindu family. If the Hindus saw him living alone with a Muslim friend, it would give them the required confidence and would probably induce them to return to their homes with courage. The Muslims, too, would be able to examine his life closely. "I have no privacy; they will see everything and find out for themselves whether I am their enemy or friend."

He did not, however, want to postpone his venture in faith till a Muslim household was ready to receive him. "When I was in detention in the Aga Khan Palace," he remarked, "I once sat down to write a thesis on India as a protagonist of non-violence. But as I proceeded with my writing, I could not go on. I had to stop. There are two aspects of Hinduism: There is, on the one hand, the historical Hinduism with its untouchability, superstitious worship of stocks and stones, animal sacrifice and so on. On the other hand, we have the Hinduism of the Gita, the Upanishads and Patanjalis *Yoga Sutra*, which is the acme of ahimsa and oneness of all creation. Ahimsa, which for me is the chief glory of Hinduism, has been sought to be explained away by our people as being meant for the *sannyasi* (saint) only. I do not think so. I hold that it is *the* way of life and India has to show it to the world. Where do I stand? Do I represent this ahimsa in my person? If I do, then the deceit and hatred that poison the atmosphere here should dissolve. It is only by going into isolation from my companions, those on whose help I have relied all along, and standing on my own crutches that I shall find my bearings and also test my faith in God."

On the 20th November, Gandhiji broke up his camp and, accompanied only by his stenographer and by Professor Nirmal Kumar Bose, his Bengali interpreter, he set out like Columbus to face the dark unknown. Before he embarked, the little group around him held a short prayer. His favourite hymn, *Vaishnavajana*, was sung. Many voices were husky, many eyes dim with tears as the tiny bamboo country-craft bearing him sailed under the arches of the Ramgunj bridge and disappeared in the distance in the direction of Srirampur. In a statement he said:

I find myself in the midst of exaggeration and falsity. I am unable to discover the truth. There is a terrible mutual distrust. Oldest friendships have snapped. Truth and Ahimsa by which I swear, and which have to my knowledge sustained me for sixty years, seem to fail to show the attributes I have ascribed to them. To test them, or better to test myself, I am going to a village called Srirampur, snapping myself from those who have been with me all these years, and who have made life easy for me. The other workers, whom I have brought with me, will each distribute themselves in other villages of Noakhali to do the work of peace, if it is at all possible, between the two communities.

I have decided to suspend all other activities in the shape of correspondence, including the work of *Harijan* and the allied weeklies.

There was, however, one consolation. Dr Rajendra Prasad sent him a wire earnestly requesting him to give up his semi-fast in view of the rapid improvement that had taken place in the Bihar situation; Gandhiji announced that he had decided to revert to normal diet as soon as his system permited. The decision came not a moment too soon. To a friend, Gandhiji wrote: "I have just been rescued from the very jaws of death."

A few days later, in a letter, he wrote: "My present mission is the most complicated and difficult one of my life. I can sing (with Cardinal Newman) with cent per cent truth: 'The night is dark and I am far from home, Lead Thou me on.' I never experienced such darkness in my life before. The night seems long. The only consolation is that I feel neither baffled nor disappointed. I am prepared for any eventuality. 'Do or Die' has to be put to test here. 'Do' here means that Hindus and Muslims should learn to live together in peace and amity. Otherwise, I should die in the attempt. It is, really, a difficult task. God's will be done."

5

THE LONE SOJOURN

After a two-and-a-half hours' journey, the slow-moving country-craft bearing the Mahatma, now separated from almost all his companions, reached Srirampur, a tiny speck of a village, and lightly he stepped out of the boat with the spring and agility of a youth to take up his solitary abode in the hut that had been prepared to receive him. Immediately, on entering it, he spread out his mattress on a wooden bedstead, which was to serve as his office by day and bed at night for the rest of his six-weeks' stay there, and arranged his books and papers at one end in his usual neat, methodical fashion. And so the new life began.

Gandhiji's new residence at Srirampur was a small tin-covered cottage, situated in a sunny clearing, in the midst of pool-dotted paddy fields and tall betel-nut and coconut groves. The bazaar and the post office were far away. All around was spread out the grim vista of destruction and desolation. Of the original 582 families in the village, 382 had been Muslim and 200 Hindu. But now only three Hindu families were left alive. The rest had all fled away in terror. The charred woodwork in the interior of the hut, just above Gandhiji's seat, bore witness to the hand of arson.

Gandhiji would have liked to live there all alone but that was hardly possible. For years he had been in the habit of taking a daily tepid immersion bath and relaxation massage as part of his treatment for high blood pressure. These were the first to be sacrificed. Instead, he rubbed a little oil over his body himself and bathed with a mug from a bucket of warm water. "It was fatiguing," he afterwards recorded in his diary, "but felt fine." The cooking of meals was reduced to the barest essentials. Half a pound of goats milk diluted with an equal volume of clear vegetable soup made up the midday meal. The same menu was served in the evening with grapefruit in addition.

The change, in spite of Gandhijis stoicism, was not effected without a wrench. His granddaughter-in-law, Abha Gandhi, had accompanied him to Noakhali. She had become an ideal nurse for him. But soon he sent her away to work under Thakkar Bapa in a village sixteen miles away. "I must own that I was getting accustomed to her service almost as a matter of habit," he wrote afterwards in a letter. "But the habit of taking service from a particular individual is inconsistent with austerity."

The news of Gandhijis departure had travelled long before him from village to village and an endless concourse of men and women had begun to trek in the direction of Srirampur from early morning. There was a continuous round of visitors the whole day. "I have come here to enter into the mind of every one of the inhabitants," Gandhiji said to one of the first persons who met him on his arrival at Srirampur. He was a Muslim *chowkidar* (watchman) from a neighbouring *badi*. He told Gandhiji that they all deplored the evil things that had happened, but what could they do? It was all the will of Allah! Gandhiji replied that he, too, believed in the omnipotence of Gods will, but individuals also had their duty to perform. He had come there to perform his.

The evening congregational prayer was attended by about a thousand persons. In the course of his prayer address, Gandhiji observed that he had advised the Hindus to depend on personal courage. But till now, he himself had lived surrounded by a number of companions. Of late, however, he had begun to say to himself: "Now is the time. If you want to know yourself, go forth alone." And so he had come practically alone to stay in their village with unquenchable faith in God, to strive and persevere till all opposition was disarmed and confidence came back to those who had lost all hope.

While having his evening walk after the prayer, he was bitten by some insect. The days diary concludes: "Excruciating pain. Weight 106½ lbs."

Hereafter his world was to consist of the poor, humble people, most of them destitutes—*malis* (gardeners), *chowkidars* and barbers, blacksmiths, weavers, carpenters, fishermen and the likes. For the time being, the world of high politics, diplomats and statesmen had been left behind. Before this, he had used politics to serve the common folk. He now set out to mould the politics of the country by rendering service to the common masses. It was a unique experiment in mass psychological engineering. He had done that before in different ways with astonishing results.

A glimpse of Gandhiji's day to day life during his sojourn at Srirampur is afforded by the detailed diary which he kept with unfailing regularity. Here are a few typical entries:

Srirampur, 21st November, 1946

Massaged the body with my own hands but had to forgo a shave (for lack of time). Had curdled milk with vegetable soup for midday meal.

22nd November, 1946

Rose at 4 am. The *Gita* recitation took two hours.

Abdullah (the Superintendent of Police) with some others came for the meeting at Ramgunj in the evening. Started at 4 pm with them for Ramgunj. Reached Ramgunj at 5.20. The meeting continued till 10.30 pm. Addressed a few words at the end. Had evening prayer on the boat, during the return journey and then some sleep. Had milk while proceeding to Ramgunj; hot water on return. Reached Srirampur at midnight.

23rd November, 1946

Visited a Muslim house at 7.30 am. Talked about the Koran to the inmates. Later they sent a present of coconuts and oranges.

Massage was given by N so that I was able to have a 40 minutes' nap on the massage table. Leafy vegetable served at midday was very bitter. Took it with 1 oz of coconut milk. Next, unsuccessfully tried to have a doze of sleep/nausea and griping. Gave myself enema. Dozed off with mud-pack on the abdomen while proceeding to Ramgunj. Had to stop the boat on account of violent diarrhoea and vomiting. Felt relieved. Reached Ramgunj at 5 pm. Had another motion during the recess but was able to address the meeting at the end without difficulty. Started on the return journey at 8.15 pm. Reached Srirampur at 11 pm. Completed the daily quota of spinning, partly on the boat while proceeding to the meeting and the balance at the meeting itself.

He had cultivated the habit of writing with the left hand in case the right hand was tired or disabled. On 2nd December, he felt exhausted but continued to work lying on his back. The diary proceeds to record: "Must stop. Even the left hand now aches and has struck work. To bed 9.30 pm."

The day sometimes extended to 16 hours of hard work. To top all this, he sometimes made incursions into the kitchen to inspect the cooking arrangements of his companions and to instruct them in culinary science in which he claimed to be an expert. He insisted on making his own bed, mended his own clothes and later even packed his travelling kit himself. The kit included practically all his personal requirements. Very often he himself wrote down the reports of his prayer addresses for the Press.

In spite of appeals to the public to spare him, the daily mail bag continued to swell. Normally, it required about half a dozen well-trained assistants to handle it. Now, he had only Professor Nirmal Kumar Bose and his stenographer. As a part of his self-denying plan, he felt he ought to deprive himself even of their secretarial assistance as far as possible. He tried to impress upon them that they must regard their desk-work as incidental; their real value to him was in the use he could make of them for the service of the riot-victims and the Muslim masses in whose midst they were. So, he took upon himself the disposal of the bulk of his mail, too.

During the disturbances, almost all the dispensaries in the affected area had been looted and destroyed. The doctors were mostly Hindus. They had fled, with the result that for miles around no medicines or medical attendance could be availed of. It gave him an opportunity to recommend to the village folk nature-cure for their simple ailments. He constituted himself into their naturopath. Before long, he had won their confidence and people began to talk of the healing touch of the man of God.

Henceforth he was more of a Noakhali man. He began taking regular lessons in Bengali and no schoolboy preparing for his examination could have worked harder or more assiduously. The lessons became a sacrament, a part of his *yajna* (act done for people's welfare or service).

Thereafter, in spite of any amount of work, he never missed his Bengali lessons. The last exercise was done on the 30th January, 1948, a few hours before the end.

* * *

The cause of Noakhali evoked universal sympathy. People from all over India were eager to help with money and materials. The Ahmadiya sect of Muslims from the Punjab sent a donation of Rs 5000. In his forwarding letter, the Secretary of the Association wrote to Gandhiji: "I have to mention in this connection that Islam stands for the assistance and emancipation of all the distressed and downtrodden, irrespective of class or creed and we consider it our sacred duty to render every possible help and cooperation for the relief of the distressed, whosoever they may be." Another cheque for Rs 650 with 200 pairs of conch bangles and a pound of vermilion (sacred powder applied by Hindu women as a mark of marriage vows) for distribution among the Hindu women who had suffered during the disturbances, came from Assam.

Gandhiji's problem was twofold. There was a danger that the riot-affected refugees might develop a mentality of dependence on public charity. This had to be prevented. At the same time, it was necessary to guard against the danger of the authorities slipping into slackness and complacency if the public took up the burden of looking after the needs of those in distress. Apart from the stigma it carried, the continued existence of the refugee camps was a headache to the authorities. But, instead of taking positive measures to create an atmosphere of security and rehabilitation, to encourage the displaced to return to their homes, the authorities tried to squeeze them out by threatening to stop distribution of free rations in the camps. Gandhiji clearly objected to the happenings. So long as an atmosphere of security was not created in the villages, arrangements for free Government relief were supposed to continue.

The case of public institutions stood on a different footing. Those who had lost everything, had a claim upon the State and the State was to provide them with vital necessities including food, clothing, shelter and medical assistance. But they would be robbing society if they accepted these without each healthy man, woman or child labouring to the extent of his or her capacity. They could ask the Government to provide them with suitable work to justify the help they were receiving.

There were about 30 organizations and half a dozen medical missions operating for relief in Noakhali. Gandhiji's standing instructions to all were for all the activities to be open and above-board. There was to be total transparency and nothing done that would give rise to insecurity or suspicion to the members of the majority community and to the authorities.

There were numerous requests from individuals and organizations from all over India, seeking permission to come and work in Noakhali. The keystone of his plan being exhibition of personal courage that comes from a living faith in God, he argued, large numbers were unnecessary. Therefore, he dissuaded all of them from coming to Noakhali. The only exception he made was in the case of a party of Indian National Army (INA) people. An ever vigilant Sardar Patel had been watching the situation that was developing in Noakhali. When, therefore, the leader of an INA group, Sardar Niranjan Singh Gill, approached him with an offer to proceed with a party of his men to Noakhali to serve under Gandhiji, he welcomed it. The presence of brave, unarmed Sikhs in the midst of riot-stricken Hindu masses might infuse courage among them. The INA had built up a fine tradition of bravery and patriotism under the leadership of Netaji Subhas Bose. They had completely banished communalism from their midst whilst they were under colours.

Gandhiji accepted the services of the INA group on condition that they should first obtain permission in writing from the Chief Minister to work in Noakhali. The Chief Minister was at first reluctant. It was very difficult for him to allow INA people to work in Noakhali, he said to Colonel Jiwan Singh, as he was already being criticized by the Muslims for allowing people from outside to work in Bengal. He read out a letter written to him by some Muslim members of the Legislative Assembly from Noakhali, accusing Gandhiji of prolonging his stay in Noakhali for a political purpose. The Chief Minister went on to say that he owed his position to the support of the Muslim League members of the Assembly. It was they who kept him in power. How could he go against their wishes? After some discussion, however, he gave his consent to their plan of work.

It was Gandhiji's expectation that, since these people had voluntarily discarded the use of arms after proving their mettle on the battlefield, they would be able to set an example of the non-violence of the strong with exceptional advantage. Sardar Patel was ready to provide the necessary finances for their upkeep, either out of Congress funds or from some other source, but Gandhiji insisted that for their financial support the INA group had to depend upon open public support by both Hindus and Muslims. The power of non-violence could not be built on money but on the faith and confidence of all the communities, including the one from which the aggressors came. Even a suspicion of financial assistance from the Congress would be fatal to his plan.

To make assurance doubly sure, he wrote to the Chief Minister that the INA people could be with him only as the accepted friends of both Hindus and Muslims. The Chief Minister was asked, therefore, to subscribe, even if it were one rupee, as a token of his approval, to the INA men's appeal for funds if he *really* approved of their activity. To Sardar Patel, he wrote:

> My conviction is hardening every day as a result of experience that an edifice built upon money tumbles down like a house of cards. Cease to put your faith in money, therefore.

A few days later, he again wrote to Sardar: "By making money our god, we dethrone God."

* * *

Slowly and steadily the leaven worked. By the end of his six weeks' stay at Srirampur, Gandhiji had won many hearts. Groups of Muslim men, women and children gathered in front of their huts with presents of fruit to greet him when he went out for his morning and evening walks. There was an instinctive recognition that he was one of them, united to them with bonds of common humanity that transcends all barriers of caste and creed.

In spite of his anxiety to be left by himself, Gandhiji could not be quite alone. His little cottage in that rather inaccessible place became like a magnet, not only to the inhabitants of the surrounding area but also to people from the remotest corners of India and even outside.

Among those who sought him out at Srirampur towards the close of his stay was M Raymond Cartier, a French journalist on his way to Indo-China. Gandhiji had read French as his second language for his London matriculation and was not a little proud of his having gone through the whole of Victor Hugo's *Les Miserables* in the original. He greeted his French visitor with a familiar *Comment allez vous?* —"How do you do ?"—and then added with loud laughter that he had exhausted his entire stock of French!

On Christmas Day, a friend brought Gandhiji a present from a woman member of the Friends Service Unit. It was a soldier's kit, containing cigarettes, socks, playing-cards, some note-paper, towels, soap, and so on. It provided Gandhiji with a light interlude. The cigarettes were kept for Pandit Nehru, who was expected to arrive after a couple of days; other articles were appropriately sent as "love-tokens" to other members of the party in different camps.

Gandhiji's rigorous self-discipline never made him intolerant of others who could not follow him in that respect. He was never censorious in his outlook. His searching eye took note of everything but never judged. Those who held him in affection were given his cooperation if they needed it in attaining self-discipline, but he did not interfere with their lives. For instance, he did not have tea or coffee, on ground of self-discipline and also as he held that they were harmful to health. He had written strongly against both, but he had them served to those who could not do without them. On one occasion, during a railway journey, he himself went out and fetched a tray of tea from the railway tea stall for his companions, while they were still sleeping. The aim was always to wean the person concerned from his weakness. But there was no compulsion except that of love.

Some members of the old Anusilan Party, a terrorist organization, came to interview him later in the day. They wanted to place their services at his disposal. One of them, Trailokya Chakravarty, told Gandhiji. that they did not know how to find an antidote to the terrible fear, which seemed to hold the people in its grip, by the method to which they had been accustomed all their lives. They felt, therefore, that it was now Gandhiji's era and not their own.

He followed it up at the evening prayer by a discourse on charity, by explaining to the congregation the celebrated verses from St Paul in which the Apostle tells the Corinthians that while all the gifts of heaven—the power of speech, the power of prophecy, the gift of healing etc—are to be prized, he can show them a way which is better than any other since it is available to all: the way of charity or love. All cannot be apostles, prophets or teachers, but all can exhibit in their lives the power of love:

I may speak in every tongue that men and angels use; yet, if I lack charity, I am no better than the clash of cymbals. I may have powers of prophecy, no secret hidden from me, no knowledge too deep for me; I may have utter faith, so that I can move mountains; yet if I lack charity, I count for nothing. I may give away all that I have, to feed the poor; I may give myself up to be burnt at the stake; if I lack charity, it goes for nothing. Charity is patient, is kind; charity feels no envy; charity is never perverse or proud, never insolent; does not claim its rights, cannot be provoked, does not brood over an injury; takes no pleasure in wrongdoing, but rejoices at the victory of truth; sustains, believes, hopes, endures, to the last. The time will come when speaking in tongues will come to an end, when knowledge will be swept away; we shall never have finished with charity.

On the last day of the dying year, two friends placed before Gandhiji a dilemma which faced them and the affected community everywhere in Noakhali. The Muslims said they were willing to receive the refugees back in their villages provided they withdrew the criminal cases arising out of the disturbances. The Hindu refugees were afraid that unless they agreed to drop the cases they would not be allowed to live in peace. To proceed with the cases would be to invite trouble. What were the workers and the riot-affected people to do? Gandhiji told the workers that there were only two alternatives before those who had committed the crimes. They could admit the crimes and justify their conduct on the ground that whatever they had done was under advice, solely for the establishment of Pakistan without any personal motive, and face the consequences. Or, they should repent and submit to the penalty of law by way of expiation. But to suggest that the cases should be dropped by way of "compromise" to facilitate the restoration of good relations between the two communities had no meaning. "I know that if the cases are proceeded with, you will be up against trouble." There may be a recrudescence of arson and murder, and at the trial the culprits may after all be acquitted. It might even lead to vendetta. But workers must be prepared to face all that. There should be no compromise out of fear. Their task was to make the villagers brave and courageous, not to make cowards of them. "They may not be able to protect the villagers' lives but they can teach them, by laying down their own lives non-violently, how to protect their honour and religion. The people may then kill and get killed, if they cannot defend themselves in a non-violent way. The workers will have done their part."

Gandhiji once defined non-violence as "uttermost purification" —purification within and without. The chief duty of a servant of the villagers, he told a gathering of workers who were engaged in rehabilitation work in Noakhali, was purification. As it was, the villages today were a festering sore on the countryside. Millions in the villages were left rotting in helpless ignorance. Clean drinking water was nowhere available, the roads were in a disgraceful condition, the waterways were choked up, the education of the villagers was neglected, their minds were steeped in darkness. Every village had more than its share of preventable diseases of all kinds. There were sharks in plenty in every village, who took the opportunity to prey upon the village-folk. The purification of this dreadful disease of the mind and the body was a task to which workers had to address themselves. India was not lacking in manpower; what was needed was collective effort, rightly directed. Bad men would not then find the environment in which they could thrive. Harmonious relations would be restored among the people when poverty and ignorance had disappeared through their cooperative effort. It was with that in mind that he had come to Noakhali and he did not mind laying down his life for it.

In this way he chose, day after day, homely little themes related to the everyday experience of common folk to illustrate deep spiritual truths and the power of non-violence or love.

6

"DO OR DIE" AT WORK

After Gandhiji left for Srirampur, the members of his party positioned themselves in about 20 villages in the affected areas.

Soon after we had settled down in our respective places, one after another, we fell ill. Butler, who in his *Erewhon* put sick men in prison and criminals in hospitals, would have found in Gandhiji a kindred spirit and an enthusiastic supporter. For Gandhiji regarded sickness as a crime. He never excused it in himself or in others.

"Come to me when you are well," wrote Gandhiji in his note to me during my illness. Accordingly, as soon as I could leave my bed, I went to Srirampur. I met him on the way to his residence while he was having his morning walk. A small dry canal spanned by a single-log *shanko* (makeshift bridge) lay across his path. These bridges, "marvels of engineering skill", as Gandhiji called them, are a specialty of East Bengal, very artistic but extremely treacherous to negotiate. They become wet and slippery due to the night dew and it demands great courage to cross them with perfect balancing skills. Gandhiji insisted on performing the feat unaided. But unable at 78 to emulate the agility of a teenager, he was saved from falling only by supporting himself on the shoulder of Nirmal Bose, who had kept himself in readiness for the emergency. A few days later, we read the following in the Press:

Gandhiji is having hard practice in balancing in attempting to cross precarious narrow bamboo bridges. For six days he failed and had to take the help of others every time. But he went on with quiet determination, (saying) "I must cross it alone." On the seventh day, to the surprise of many, Gandhiji succeeded in crossing that betel-nut tree pole. His daily practice repeated four times, however, continues. He would say, "I shall (feel) confident (only) when I attain perfection so that I can cross (even longer) bridges of this type."

That day, he poured out his mind. In spite of his exhortations, the exodus of refugees from East Bengal continued. Everywhere there was a demand for more and more military and police protection. He was insistent that they must not rely at all on the police or the military for their protection if they valued independence. What was the substitute for police and military protection? He had propagated the strength of ahimsa. It was a novel suggestion and it only mystified them. But they were in a continuous sceptical state. How could he blame them? Had he made it good in his own case?

"I am in the midst of a raging fire, and will not leave till it is put out," he remarked to Dr Amiya Chakravarty of the Calcutta University, who had come to see him.

Dr Chakravarty asked him what should be the technique for approaching the wrongdoers, so that their resistance would dissolve. "They are not only unrepentant but defiant and even jubilant over their misdeeds."

The only way to meet their attitude, replied Gandhiji, was not to succumb to it but to live in their midst and retain one's sense of truth.

Goodness must be joined with knowledge. Mere goodness is not of much use. One must retain the fine discriminating quality which goes with spiritual courage. One must know, in a crucial situation, when to speak and when to be silent, when to act and when to refrain from it.

The new basis of life has to be built here in the villages where Hindus and Muslims have lived and suffered together on the land of their forefathers and must live together in future. I have come to live in their midst and share their tasks, to cement the two together or to perish in the attempt.

Dr Chakravarty suggested that, "Noakhali has become a laboratory, where a crucial test is being experimented; the remedy will apply to situations all over the world where disputes arise between communities and nationalities and a new technique is needed for peaceful adjustment."

Gandhiji remarked, "That makes us responsible all the more; our work has to ring true. For me," he continued, "if this thing is pulled through, it will be the crowning act of my life."

"I am still groping," remarked Gandhiji when I saw him a week later. "Here I am, out to perform a stupendous *yajna,* but my unfitness for the task is showing at every step. There can, however, be no running away."

To another friend, he remarked: "I don't want to return defeated from Bengal. I would rather die, if need be, at the hands of an assassin. But I do not want to court it, much less do I wish it."

* * *

The still was still volcanic when we took up our stations in our respective villages. There were seven of us in Gandhiji's party: Amtus Salam, a Muslim inmate of the Ashram, who had become Gandhiji's adopted daughter; Sushila Pai, a graduate of the Bombay University and one of Gandhiji's secretarial aids; Kanu Gandhi, the grand-nephew of Gandhiji, and his wife Abha; Prabhudas, a young man who used to be an office assistant; my sister, Dr Sushila Nayar and I. Most of these villages had been partly or completely deserted by their Hindu inhabitants. The Hindus who had not fled had been forcibly converted. Their womenfolk dared not open their lips to us about the ordeal they had gone through, except in the privacy of their inner apartments. They were still scared to put on their foreheads the auspicious vermilion mark. On their wrists they stopped wearing conch-shell bangles, the other auspicious symbol which is worn in Bengal by all married Hindu women. These had been forcibly removed by those who had converted them. In some cases, the women had themselves removed them out of fear. Their faces were pinched and pale and there was a scared, haunted animal look in their eyes.

At the time of our arrival in our respective villages, there was a general feeling of revulsion among the Muslims, against the recent happenings. The older set appeared to be sincerely unhappy with the past and sometimes even recalled with tears the times when Hindus and Muslims used to live together like brothers. They blamed the "young hot-heads" and their "newfangled doctrines", as they put it, for what had happened. Such things had never been heard of before in those parts, they said. What was the world coming to! Those who had actually taken part in the disturbances generally denied that "anything" had happened! Even lads of 10 and 12 had the same uniform pattern of prevarication on their lips. It was the nearest approach to mass perjury and regimentation of a whole coming generation in the psychology of untruth.

* * *

The refugees who were repatriated to their villages were provided with a week's ration. The scene which awaited them on their return was one of indescribable desolation. The homesteads were in ruins, at some places even without roofs, doors or window frames. The yards of the *badis* were littered with dirt and debris, broken earthen pots, pieces of quilt and torn dirty clothing. Heaps of coconut shells and husk, and rusty trunks that had been broken open and rifled during the disturbances lay everywhere. The backyards and environs were overgrown with rank vegetation, which in Noakhali swallows up everything. The ponds were choked with weeds, their embankments dilapidated and walks and footpaths in a sorry state as a result of long neglect and the inundations caused by the last rains. The orchards and coconut and betel-nut gardens were denuded of fruit.

We were all of us men and women of ordinary clay—very crude and imperfect instruments for the unique experiment which Gandhiji had launched in the application of the power of non-violence or soul. It was an unprecedented situation. We were driven by our deep love and loyalty to him and faith in his ideals. We lacked his power of penance, gained from the ceaseless sustained practice of the five cardinal spiritual disciplines. We were well aware of our shortcomings and were sincerely trying in soldierly obedience to carry out his instructions in letter and spirit to the best of our abilities. All we could claim was that some of the results obtained were astounding and provided enough experience of what can be achieved when even a small modicum of the great principle which he taught is realized in practice.

* * *

Thakkar Bapa, the champion of "lost causes", was an institution in himself. He had accompanied Gandhiji to Noakhali and set up his camp at Haimchar, in the heart of the Harijan area in Charmandal. About the same age as Gandhiji, just like Gandhiji, he seemed to grow younger with the years. Unremitting toil in the service of humanity was his undying passion. His simple habits, poised dignity and force of character made a deep impression on the Muslim elders of the locality, while his level-headedness and passion for precision —the outcome of his probationership in the Servants of India Society —won him the esteem of the Government officials who soon learnt to respect his formidable array of facts and figures.

Thakkar Bapa remained at his post throughout Gandhiji's stay in Noakhali and even later. When his institutional obligations called him back to Delhi, he continued to serve the cause of Noakhali from there with the same zeal and devotion.

Sushila Pai's camp was set up at Karpara. It became a rallying centre, especially for the women. She set up as a schoolmistress, held daily prayer meetings and gatherings for women and young girls in her area to overcome their fear. As a result of her initiative, the local school that had closed down during the disturbances was reopened. She also succeeded in getting the local weekly bazaar reopened. To encourage others, she set up a stall herself. She earned the love and respect of even the Muslims, who came to her for help and advice and even asked her to mediate in their disputes.

Sucheta Kripalani utilized her talent for relieving the destitution around her. Brave as a lioness, she made herself feared and respected.

Last but not least among the band of workers in Noakhali was Sadhan Bose. He distinguished himself by his gentleness, renunciation and purity. His devout religious nature particularly fitted him for the work of organizing the women. He refused to come out of Noakhali even after Gandhiji's death and died at his post six years later, fully living up to Gandhiji's mantra, "Do or Die".

The workers helped create an atmosphere of courage, self-reliance and hope in and around their respective camps, and enabled a beginning to be made in the rehabilitation of the riot victims in their original homes, in spite of the Bengal Government's halting policy, the latent hostility of the local Muslims and the unsatisfactory attitude of the Muslim League. But they were few and scattered over widely separated places and the tide was running fast against them. The overall picture in Noakhali continued to be gloomy.

* * *

The plan of Government-sponsored Peace Committees proved to be ill-fated.

No action was taken by the authorities when a Peace Committee submitted a unanimous list of undesirable characters that needed to be rounded up. In another place, whenever a complaint was lodged, the *thana* officer passed on the information to the local Muslim League organization, from where, within a few hours, it reached the persons complained against, exposing the complainants to threats of vendetta and reprisals.

Gandhiji addressed a letter to the Chief Minister of Bengal, drawing his attention to the growing deterioration in the situation:

Somehow or the other, the Committees have failed to inspire confidence. In spite of all my efforts, the exodus continues and very few persons have returned to their villages. They say, the guilty parties are still roaming freely, sporadic cases of murder and arson still continue, the abducted women have not all been returned, burnt houses are not being rebuilt and generally, the atmosphere of goodwill is lacking.

Quoting from a letter, he gave details:

Economic boycott is going on throughout the sub-division. Muslim boatmen do not carry Hindus. Hindus are not getting Muslim labourers to reap their paddy etc. In most cases, Muslims do not purchase any commodity from Hindu shopkeepers in the Chandpur sub-division. Throughout the sub-division, Hindu fishermen are not allowed to catch fish. Sometimes they are beaten, sometimes their nets are taken away.

This is by no means an exhaustive catalogue. I do not know whether you have an adequate conception of the mischief done.

The Chief Minister's letter, which crossed Gandhiji's, brought among other things, the following:

I appreciate very much your desire to bring about peace between Hindus and Muslims in Bengal, (but) the Muslims feel that if you really wish to pursue your objective of establishing good fellowship, Bihar should be the real field. Your stay has encouraged many of your volunteers to manufacture evidence and place it before you and to carry on persecution of the local Muslims, particularly the local Muslim League leaders, which will not possibly lead to mutual confidence in the future.

The military and the police have pervaded the villages and you must have heard of their excesses. Muslims have been indiscriminately arrested and assaulted, their women have been molested and outraged, their houses have been looted and a reign of terror has been introduced. All the important Muslims are being implicated, such as Presidents of Union Boards, Members of School Boards, *maulvis*, maulanas, headmasters, even MLAs—all persons, in fact, who may be considered respectable. The purpose is only too clear. Revenge through the process of law and revenge on the innocents. If you really want friendliness and mutual toleration, this kind of legal persecution has to cease.

The ugly truth of the matter was that the *maulvis*, maulanas, headmasters, MLAs—in fact, persons belonging to all these classes that might be considered "respectable", as the Chief Minister had put it, had taken active part in unlawful activities before, during and after the disturbances. If the military and the police had misbehaved, the Ministry should have taken action against them; after all, they were the servants of the Crown. But here was the Chief Minister finding fault with the riot victims instead, for invoking the law against their powerful and well-placed oppressors and using it as a plea for asking Gandhiji to terminate his mission in Noakhali!

In the Chief Minister's next letter, Noakhali had completely faded out of the picture. The letter was devoted exclusively to reports of happenings in Bihar!

Replying to the Chief Minister, Gandhiji wrote:

I note that you have repeated the advice you have given me often enough that my place is in Bihar rather than in Noakhali. If I felt that my presence was at all necessary in Bihar, I assure you that I would not need any encouragement from you to go there. You will pardon me for not taking your statements for gospel truth.

Throughout his life, it had been a source of perennial satisfaction to Gandhiji that he had generally been able to retain the affection and trust of those whose principles and policy he had had to oppose. But here that solace seemed to fail him.

After much thought and self-introspection, he wrote a personal letter to the Chief Minister, addressing him as "My dear Shaheed," and signing it as "Yours, Bapu."

I remind you of our pleasant meeting in Faridpur. If I remember rightly, you were the only one sitting in front of me spinning assiduously, though you were unable to pull an even or fine thread. And then, when I applied to you some distant adjective of affection, you corrected me by saying that you felt as a son to me. I would like to think that you are still the same Shaheed and to feel proud that my son has become Chief Minister of Bengal.

You seem to believe the stories of Bihar cruelties with which you have been regaled. I frankly confess to you that these reports do not carry conviction to me. If even 50 per cent of the stories are true, life would become a burden for me. You should know that though here, I was able to affect events in Bihar by putting myself on a fat-free diet and by my proposal, if things did not mend, to undertake complete fast.

But it was no use. It was to a mind hardened by prejudice and deep suspicion that his words were addressed.

What was Gandhiji to do? It was certainly true that what had happened in Bihar was brutal enough and deserved the severest condemnation. But he argued with himself that he could exercise his personal influence in Bihar even from a distance; the Bihar Ministers were his friends, his word carried weight with them. His partial fast and notice of a complete one had already had a magical effect. There was nothing more he could do by going there. But he could not use that weapon in the case of Noakhali, where the Muslim League organization and a large section of the Muslims regarded him as an enemy of Islam. He had still not won their confidence.

Insofar as the Muslim League was concerned, he had come to a dead-end. There was nothing further he could do on the political plane, short of surrendering his principle. But in Noakhali there was a lot to be done amongst the masses of Hindus and Muslims. Their needs were the same, their difficulties and problems were alike and admitted of a common solution. He would go and live in their midst, become one with them, share their life and make them share his. He would teach them to overcome ignorance, poverty and disease, and inculcate in them faith in and worship of one God, who is the same for both Hindus and Muslims. When he had thus entered into their minds and helped them to enter his, perhaps a time would come when the atmosphere changed.

"It is quite clear to me," he declared, "my word carries very little weight. Distrust has gone too deep for exhortation." As soon as water in the rice-fields dried up, and his arrangements were completed, he would set out on foot on a village-to-village tour to take the message of goodwill and peace from door to door. He would not return to the village from which he started. There would be no time limit. He would share the life of the villagers and become one of them. He would proceed with as few companions as possible on his march and preferably stay in the houses of Muslim friends. He would like to go absolutely unprotected, for everybody to see that in his heart he had nothing but love and friendship for the Muslims.

7

THE BAREFOOT PILGRIM

The village of Srirampur and its environs were beginning to stir into new life when, on the morning of 2nd January, 1947, winding up his camp, Gandhiji set out on his long trek. The rice crop had recently been harvested and the paddy fields lay bare. The whole countryside was astir. On either side of the way, villagers from both the communities stood lined up to have a look at the Mahatma as he passed by.

Sixteen years earlier, he had set out on foot similarly, on his historic Salt March to the sea, with a party of 79. Back then, he used to walk eight to ten miles daily and he outpaced many a youngster without being tired. The physical frame had since been worn out by many long fasts and a decade and a half of ceaseless toil; but the spirit within burnt stronger than ever. In those days, people used to join him in thousands in his march and were welcome; this time he let it be known to all concerned that he wanted no other companion but God in his pilgrimage.

Abdullah, the Superintendent of Police, who had developed a deep attachment for Gandhiji and had become almost a member of the family, accompanied him from Srirampur to Chandipur.

The evening prayer was held at the rather early hour of 4.30, to enable the women who had come from the neighbouring village to attend the prayer meeting to return home before dark. Gandhiji remarked that he would roam from village to village, teach the villagers how to clean their ponds and practise arts and crafts that would enrich their lives. Such unselfish labour of love was bound to ultimately overcome all prejudice.

In one of his post-prayer addresses, Gandhiji compared his venture in Noakhali to a pilgrimage. In ancient days, pilgrimages were undertaken on foot. The most sacred places were situated at the far and inaccessible ends of India. The journey to them was long and arduous. During the journey the pilgrims walked barefoot, put themselves under rigorous vows and practised austerity. The merit of the pilgrimage lay in self-purification. In the context of his mission in Noakhali this meant that all impurities should be removed from their hearts, "most of all the impurity styled fear". If those who had suffered during the riots could shed their fear, they would want not punishment or revenge, but the conversion of their assailants. By cultivating in themselves the spirit of fearlessness and forgiveness, all could join him in his pilgrimage without leaving their homes.

Rehabilitation was, to Gandhiji, not merely economic, but moral and spiritual as well. There had to be a spiritual rebirth. And not only theirs but their oppressors' as well. To the sufferers, his advice was that they should forget all about the culprits, return to their homes and face all risks.

And even while he was energetically pursuing his mission of peace in Noakhali, where the Hindus were the victims, his heart ached no less for the Muslims of Bihar. In answer to his inquiries, a Minister from Bihar with several representative officials was sent by the Bihar Government to apprise him of the situation in Bihar. They admitted that the brutality had taken place during the disturbances. They were prepared, they said, to bear all justifiable censure on that account.

* * *

In Noakhali nature is kind. The earth under the feet is soft and soothing. There are no sharp stones or thorns to prick bare feet. Even the stubble in the harvested fields is soft as silk. Gandhiji had very delicate feet. He took extraordinary care of them. Even then, he was footsore when he arrived at Chandipur. But he decided that he would have no footwear during the rest of his wanderings; it would be an act of irreverence on his part to tread the ground which was hallowed by the sufferings of innocent men and women, with shoes on.

His travelling kit included practically everything he required, from pen, pencil and paper to needle and sewing thread for mending clothes; a few cooking-pots, an earthen bowl and a wooden spoon, a galvanized iron bucket for bath, a commode, a hand-basin, and soap; and last but not least, the spinning-wheel and its accessories. In addition to these there were files, papers and a few books. A portable typewriter completed the office equipment. The books carried in the bag included:

1. *The Sayings of Muhammad*
2. *The World Bible*
3. *A Book of Jewish Thoughts*
4. *Dhammapada*
5. *Sukhamani Saheb* (the Sikh Scripture)
6. *Shri Ramacharitamanas*
7. *Discovery of India*
8. *Ashram Bhajanavali*
9. *Gitanjali*
10. *The Bhagavad Gita*

On 7th January, his last night at Chandipur, he woke up at 2 am and, with his characteristic thoroughness, inquired to make sure if his instructions for the march had all been carried out. At the morning prayer he asked for his favourite *Vaishnavajana* hymn to be sung with this variation that for *Vaishnavajana* in the refrain, *Muslim-jana, Parsi-jana,* and *Christian-jana* were to be substituted by turns as a mark of identification with the followers of all faiths.

The disc of the rising sun had just begun to peer above the horizon when, at 7.30, he set out on his journey singing Tagore's celebrated song "Walk Alone":

> If they answer not to thy call, walk alone;
> If they are afraid and cower mutely facing the wall,
> O thou of evil luck,
> Open thy mind and speak out alone.
> If they turn away and desert you when crossing the wilderness,
> O thou of evil luck,

trample the thorns under thy tread,
and along the blood-lined track travel alone.

If they do not hold up the light
when the night is troubled with storm,
O thou of evil luck,
with the thunder-flame of pain ignite thine own heart
and let it burn alone.

The singing of one variation after another of *Ramadhun* was kept up all along the way.

The route lay through a landscape of enchanting beauty. A narrow footpath, over which two persons could hardly walk abreast, wound sinuously through colonnades of stately palms, whose straight-growing stems and drooping branches were reflected in the glassy surface of the ponds by the side of which they grew.

Finding suitable accommodation for Gandhiji, everyday during his one-day-one-village tour, was a problem. Satish Das Gupta thought he could get round it by the device of the portable hut. But what use was accommodation if the hearts were shut? So Gandhiji declined the use of the folding hut and camped in a damp school-shed instead. "If there is no one to receive me under his roof, I shall be happy to rest under the hospitable shade of a tree."

At the evening prayer meeting, a number of Muslims were also present. But as soon as *Ramadhun* began, some of them walked out. It saddened him that they could not tolerate God being remembered by any other name except Khuda or Allah. In the course of his prayer discourse, he remarked that while he was very careful not to wound unnecessarily the susceptibility of anyone and had come to Noakhali to demonstrate his friendship for the Muslims by staying in their midst and serving them, he could not possibly give up *Ramanama*, which was food for his soul. It was the same Creator that people worshipped through many tongues.

A piercing, chilly wind was blowing the next morning when Gandhiji reached the village of Fatehpur. As Manu applied oil to his feet, she noticed that they were bleeding. Gandhiji's Muslim host at

Fatehpur, Maulvi Ibrahim, was a remarkable character in his own way. For the last 50 years he had been trying to induce the Muslims to take to various occupations which they had shunned as being "low class". They would not fish, so he took to fishing himself; they would not weave, he set up looms and succeeded in starting a weaving school which became quite popular.

The evening prayer at Fatehpur was attended by a large number of local Muslims. The Muslim part of the audience sat throughout the whole meeting and Maulvi Ibrahim took part in it and spoke affectionately about the programme.

In Char Krishnapur, which Gandhiji visited next, the bulk of the population consisted of Namashudras (Harijans). They had suffered terribly and the terror had reigned long after other parts had been relieved.

In contrast with the preceding stages of the journey, where the population was predominantly Muslim, the entire route to Char Krishnapur was lined by eager crowds. The prospective host of Gandhiji, there too, was a Muslim, but he had changed his mind at the eleventh hour as, he said, he felt helpless in the face of the pressure of a section of the Muslims. Accommodation for Gandhiji, in consequence, had to be found in a low-roofed shelter improvised from charred, corrugated sheets salvaged from a burnt-down homestead. To keep off the heat, it was covered with green twigs. Still, it was oppressively warm and stuffy inside.

In the course of a conversation with a friend, Gandhiji remarked: "I do not want to die of a creeping paralysis of my faculties. I would love to fade out doing my duty with my last breath." One of his letters to a friend described him as, "trekking over unfurrowed tracks in stormy weather."

To Gandhiji, the test of a good worker was whether he knew how to match his work to the human material and the resources available at the moment and to fit his particular bit into the larger plan. A sound rule was to pick out a few items that were within one's reach and capacity and work them out in detail, while keeping the whole in view.

Gandhiji literally believed in the dictum that one can serve the whole universe by doing one's allotted task steadfastly and well, and that it is better for one to die while performing one's own immediate duty than to allow oneself to be lured away by the prospect of the "distant scene", however attractive.

* * *

While the stalemate in Noakhali continued thus, the pressure on Gandhiji to go to Bihar went on increasing. On the 6th February, 1947, he wrote to Jawaharlal Nehru: "Very great pressure is being put upon me to go to Bihar, because they all say that things are not properly represented to me on behalf of the Bihar Government. I am watching."

There was not a day but brought a sheaf of letters—angry letters, threatening letters, sometimes even abusive letters—mostly from the Muslim Leaguers, wanting to know why Gandhiji did not go to Bihar. He carefully examined each one of them for any grain of truth that might have been in it and had all allegations checked up by the Bihar Government and others till they were either substantiated or proved incorrect.

While thus refusing to allow himself to be influenced by anger or ridicule, Gandhiji continued his effort to get to the truth. He encouraged Colonel Niranjan Singh Gill of the Indian National Army to proceed to Bihar and report. Though Gill's report exploded many a myth propagated by the Muslim League, it was damaging enough to the Bihar Government. It set Gandhiji thinking. In a letter to Dr Syed Mahmud, the Bihar Minister, he wrote: "I cannot decide between Muslim League reports and what is reported to me from other sources as to where lies the truth. I want you to write to me how far the League report is true." Dr Mahmud kept silent. His continued silence in spite of repeated reminders from Gandhiji was intriguing. It made Gandhiji impatient to get to the truth.

* * *

Gandhiji began to make plans for the third phase of his pilgrimage on foot. But man proposes, God disposes.

The following day, Dr Mahmud's secretary arrived with a letter from the former. It was a long letter, full of anguish. It reiterated that at the root of the communal problem lay the Muslim fear that they would be wiped out if the Hindus came to power. "I used to tell the British before," Dr Mahmud's letter continued, "if you do not settle with India in Gandhiji's lifetime, you will live to regret it afterwards. In the same way today I tell the Indian Muslims that if they do not settle the communal question in your lifetime, it will never be settled. That opportunity seems almost to have slipped by. But maybe even now if you come, the Hindus might be brought to repentance and the situation still saved."

The most painful part of it was that if facts were stated, Congressmen could not be absolved of blame. There were stories of unspeakable barbarities having been perpetrated upon Muslims. "I and several women besides me," recorded one of Gandhiji's party afterwards, "could hardly restrain our tears. Bapu sank into deep thought. Poor Mujtaba Saheb (Dr Mahmud's secretary), he could not proceed with the reading of the letter. The moment he had finished, Bapu sent a wire to the Chief Minister of Bihar to ask if he could start for Bihar: 'Dr Syed Mahmud and others would like me to visit Bihar. Do you feel likewise? Please tell me what you feel.' "

In the evening, Gandhiji announced at the prayer gathering his decision to proceed to Bihar. He referred to the report which he had received about the atrocities that were said to have been committed by the Hindus of Bihar. In comparison to this, the happenings of Noakhali seemed "to pale into insignificance". He could not resist Dr Mahmud's call. He was as concerned about the welfare of the Muslims as about that of the Hindus. He had sent an urgent wire to the Chief Minister of Bihar and it was highly likely that it might be their last meeting for the time being. The word he wanted to leave with them for the short time that he expected to be away would be that they should live together as brothers. They would be able to do that only if on either side they were prepared to lay down their lives without retaliation, in defence of what they considered sacred.

No reply from the Bihar Chief Minister came even on the following day. Before going to sleep at night, Gandhiji gave directions that the luggage was to be kept ready for the journey next day. Among the things which he kept specially prepared to be taken with him were a *Bengali Teacher* and a Bengali dictionary, and a notebook in which he did his daily writing exercise in Bengali. The daily Bengali lesson was to him like the call to prayer. He also kept up the practice of having a Bengali devotional song sung during the morning prayer. Far away in Bihar, it brought back to him the call of the Noakhali jungles, the travail of the poor in their humble huts, whom he had left behind, and his "Do or Die" promise to them.

From early morning next day, Gandhiji's camp was astir. The air was tense with anxiety. The wrench of separation was on every face. A heavy pall of mist hung over the place. Only the dull patter from the dripping forest leaves broke the silence. At 11 am, the fog lifted and the sun peered through. But the gloom within deepened with the approach of the hour of departure. At last everything was ready for the journey. A number of colleagues and co-workers had come from various centres to bid goodbye and receive final instructions. The most active of them all was the 78-year-old Thakkar Bapa. With his precise, methodical habits, he did not rest till he had satisfied himself by a personal inspection that everything had been done according to plan and all the luggage got safely into the jeep. At last Gandhiji emerged from his hut. For the first time after two months he was again seen wearing sandals.

The party reached Chandpur at 3.20 pm and the quiet peace of the last four months gave place to the din and bustle of congested city life once more. Swarming crowds followed him in the evening to the riverside where his last public prayer meeting in East Bengal was held. It was attended by nearly 30,000.

Addressing the mammoth gathering, Gandhiji said that the same reason that had brought him to Noakhali was now taking him to Bihar. He was sorry that he had turned a deaf ear earlier to the pressing requests made to him by Muslim friends to go to Bihar. He had flattered himself with the belief that he would be able to affect the Bihar Hindus from his place in Bengal. But Dr Mahmud's letter had shown him the necessity of proceeding to Bihar. He expected to return to his chosen scene of service—Noakhali—as soon as possible.

A member of the audience asked how those who had lost their dear ones or their homes, which had taken long years of sweat and sacrifice, could forgive and forget. How could they bring themselves to look with a feeling of brotherhood upon the community from which the hooligans came?

The way to forget and forgive, replied Gandhiji, was to contemplate Bihar, which had done much worse things than Noakhali. Did they want the Muslims of Bengal to take revenge for the Hindu atrocities in Bihar? He was sure they did not. From that they were to learn to forget and forgive.

At 9.30 pm the party boarded the steamer. Huge crowds had gathered at the jetty, too. The last to take leave was Colonel Jiwan Singh. He stayed on in Noakhali even after Gandhiji's death and added a footnote to the story of the relations between India and Pakistan.

From Goalando, the party proceeded by train.

* * *

In spite of the secrecy that had been observed to detrain him at Fatwa—18 miles from Patna—the usual contingent of newspaper reporters was there at the railway station.

Out of the thronging crowd on the platform, Gandhiji's eye picked out Dr Syed Mahmud and Professor Abdul Bari, the Muslim President of the Provincial Congress Committee, both of them old colleagues and staunch nationalists. "So, you are still alive!" he remarked with an attempt at a dry, joyless laugh than which nothing could be sadder.

Dr Rajendra Prasad, with members of the Bihar Ministry and the Provincial Congress Committee, met him at Dr Mahmud's residence as soon as Gandhiji reached there. As Gandhiji sat surrounded by his veteran lieutenants, his head was bowed. All was not well with Bihar. The leaders were apologetic. They had done all they could and would do all he might ask them to do. But that was a poor consolation for what had already happened. Dr Rajendra Prasad had told him that genuine repentance was lacking. In Bihar, Bengal and the rest of India there was a belief that Bihar had "saved" Bengal. The gloom on Gandhiji's face deepened.

Dr Rajendra Prasad told him about the reports of the economic boycott of the Muslims who held almost all the minor professions. In the weddings of Brahmins, Muslim peddlers supplied the bangles. Likewise, the barbers were Muslims. Without them no marriage could be celebrated. It was they who supplied flowers for worship. To separate the two communities when their lives were so much interlinked was like tearing apart the limbs of a living person.

Soon after, Gandhiji had another long meeting with the Bihar Ministers. "We should make a public confession of our mistake," he told them. No commission of inquiry had been appointed to date. "If we are not quick about the matter, it will lose its effect. If we do not appoint a commission, we shall be held to have admitted the League's case." The Chief Minister, Srikrishna Sinha, expressed the fear that the League would make political capital out of it. Gandhiji admitted that it was not improbable. But justice never paused to consider if it would be exploited. "My 60 years' experience has taught me nothing if not that."

The Chief Minister put in that they had never tried to "minimize" the atrocities. That touched off Gandhiji's pent up feeling. "From what I have been hearing, it seems to me that the Bihar massacre was like the Jallianwala Bagh massacre."

At last the day of painful heart-searching came to a close. It was time for the evening prayer. There was a mammoth gathering. Muslims were present in large numbers. Many ladies in purdah also attended the prayer.

He had misled himself with the belief, Gandhiji said, that it would be unnecessary for him to visit what he had affectionately called *his* Bihar. It was, however, no use crying over spilt milk. He hoped that they would do all reparation possible which must in its magnitude be as great as their crime, if their repentance was real. If they adopted an attitude of self-righteousness by putting it all on the goondas, for whom the Bihar Congressmen could not be held responsible, they would reduce the Congress to a miserable political party instead of being the one national organization which, by right of service, claimed to represent the whole of India. To make good that claim, the Congress must hold itself responsible for the misdeeds of all communities and classes. That many Congressmen had staked their lives in order to save their Muslim brethren was no answer to the charge that was justly levelled at the Bihar Hindus by indignant and injured Muslims.

He was grieved to find that there were thoughtless Hindus in all parts of India who falsely hugged the belief that Bihar was able to bring to a halt the mischief that the Muslims in Bengal had let loose.

It was cowardice to believe that barbarity such as India had of late witnessed could ever protect a people's culture, religion or freedom. He made bold to say that wherever of late there had been such cruelty, it had its origin in cowardice, and cowardice is never redeemed for an individual or a nation. The way to take reprisals, therefore, was not to copy the barbarous deeds of Noakhali but to confront barbarism with manliness, which consisted in daring to die without a thought of retaliation and without compromising one's honour.

* * *

Several influential local Muslims came to see Gandhiji the next day. They had all suffered heavily during the disturbances. Trying to laugh away their grief, he told them that they should put behind them their own misfortunes, and get ready to proceed to Noakhali to engage themselves there as he was engaging himself in Bihar.

Bihar was the land of the Ramayana, Gandhiji remarked at the evening prayer meeting. Howsoever uneducated or poor a Bihari might be, his heart vibrated to the music of that great epic. They knew what sin was and what constituted merit. The misdeeds they were guilty of were of terrible proportions. Should not their atonement, too, be of the same order? It was in that spirit that they were to approach those who had suffered during the riots, and try to do the right thing by them. He had said the previous evening that all Muslim women, who were alleged to be confined in Hindu homes, were to be returned. The looted property was to be returned to its owners and the losses compensated for.

Mohammad Yunus, an old friend, came to see Gandhiji. In reply to the question as to how long he expected to be in Bihar, Gandhiji said that he had set no time limit. Islam had not yet forgotten the Karbala, where brother's arm was raised against brother, although it had happened 1300 years ago. How could he forget his Karbala, that was Bihar?

8

THE VEIL LIFTED

What had happened? What had made the "mild Bihari" turn berserk so that he could indulge in cold-blooded butchery of women and children?

With a few notable exceptions, Bihar, as a province, had always been the most peaceful. Some of the Bihar Congress leaders, notably Dr Rajendra Prasad, were respected by Muslims and Hindus alike. The Congress and the Khilafat Movements in the 1920s had further improved communal relations. But a change gradually came over the scene. Communalism was captured by reaction in the struggle against the rising tide of democracy.

In 1939, the Congress Ministers resigned as a protest against the insult to Indian self-respect of India being declared by the British power a belligerent country in the Second World War without her consent. The Muslim League celebrated the event by observing a "Deliverance Day"! As the tension mounted, a feeling of exasperation took hold of the Hindus at what they considered to be the unpatriotic attitude of the Muslim League. They read from day to day all sorts of threats by the leaders of the League to achieve Pakistan by force. There were scurrilous attacks in the Muslim League Press on Hindu religion and practices. The "Hindus" and the "Hindu Congress" were frequently referred to as "our enemies". All this had a very unfortunate repercussion on the Hindu mass mentality all over India, particularly in Bihar.

Then came 1942. The Hindu masses of Bihar had to bear the brunt of repression. The opposition of the League to the "Quit India"

Movement further widened the gulf between the communities in Bihar. This created a feeling in the Hindu masses in Bihar, as elsewhere, that the Muslim League was a barrier to the freedom of their country. They denounced the League as a tool of British power.

* * *

The Calcutta "Direct Action" of August, 1946 set up a double shock wave, one travelling in the direction of Noakhali, the other in that of Bihar. More than a million Biharis earned their livelihood in Calcutta as shopkeepers, rickshaw-pullers, door-keepers etc. The events in Calcutta had resulted in the killing of a large number of them. There is in Bihar a large Bengali Hindu population. The relatives of many of them were also killed in Calcutta. The survivors of those killed or otherwise affected in Calcutta streamed as refugees into Bihar. They spread out in the rural areas carrying stories gruesome by themselves, sometimes exaggerated.

On top of this came the news of Noakhali. Accounts of forcible conversion of large numbers of people, abduction and rape inflame passions anywhere. The Hindu sentiment is particularly sensitive to crimes against womanhood. The Biharis became terribly excited.

The systematic programme of arson, murder and rape of one community by the other as a political weapon, with what looked like the undeclared help of the Muslim League Government of Bengal, had so shocked the popular mind that the wildest stories found ready credence. There gradually grew up in the Congress a section which, without daring openly to go against the official policy of the Congress, secretly sympathized with the counter-communalism of the Hindus that was coming into existence.

* * *

The Bihar disturbances demonstrated that democracy without proper political education of the electorate is like a house built on sand. Freedom of speech is a dangerous instrument when the masses are ignorant. Led astray, they hold the government, which is their servant, in their grip. Secondly, when the majority turns against the minority, no government, least of all a democratic one, can save it. It is impossible to put an armed constable at the disposal of each individual. And when the poison spreads, government servants are as likely to be affected by it as others. They can then, with all the more impunity, defy the impartial policies of the government. No democratic government can afford to dismiss all its officers or shoot all the people. Gandhiji had, therefore, to say in Noakhali that if the majority community did not want the minority to remain in their midst, he would have no alternative but to ask them to migrate. The minority can remain in the midst of the majority only by winning the latter's friendship. Hence, those who taught the minority to regard the majority as their "enemies" and severed the age-long link of friendship between the two, lightly played with the lives of millions. The third important lesson of the riot was that the government machinery had become wooden. Even in normal times it moved at a snail's pace. In an emergency, it proved to be altogether inadequate.

When Gandhiji arrived in Bihar in March, 1947, the Hindu masses had sobered down. Congressmen, after they had recovered their bearings, did some splendid work. The quick suppression of the riot was considerably due to their efforts. They were also responsible for saving thousands of Muslims, sometimes even at the risk of their own lives. But the campaign of calumny by the League against the Congress and the Hindus, and the general atmosphere of communal hatred which prevailed in the refugee camps, had soured the hearts of a section of the Congressmen and made them indifferent to the fate of the Muslims.

The majority of the Hindus were still unrepentant. Many of their breadwinners were in jail. The Congress had condemned what they had done. They were consequently in a sullen mood. Stolen property was not returned. Economic boycott of Muslims had come into operation at places. Their crops were cut and carried away. Even the door-leaves from the deserted houses were removed. Stray incidents of harassment continued. The general attitude of the Hindu public was one of indifference to such incidents.

The Muslims were still in the grip of fear and its concomitant hatred, full of mistrust of the Government, the Congress and the Hindu community in general.

The scene to which Gandhiji came was thus chaotic and full of violence. He had to lead people to introspection and self-examination;

to turn hardened hearts to genuine repentance; to steady friends and win over foes, even against what they mistook for their self-interest; to put heart into those who had been shaken by their sufferings and to bring love where hatred and cunning ruled; and finally, to call a mighty organization that had forgotten itself, back to the path of duty, and thereby steady the foundations of democracy shaking at its very inception. His non-violence was called to the supreme test. Bihar became another outpost in his "Do or Die" mission.

* * *

Gandhiji set out for the interior to carry his voice directly to the people in the villages and, as he put it, to "read in the face of the countryside" the mystery of what had happened.

The first village to be visited was Kumarhar, three miles from the Patna railway station. Gandhiji was deeply moved when an old man with a long white beard led him through the ruins and showed him the damage done to his house and the houses of his relatives. Even the library and the mosque had not been spared. Desecrating places of worship always pained Gandhiji deeply and he used some very strong words to give expression to his feeling in his post-prayer speech. They could not put forward the plea, he said, that the Muslims had desecrated Hindu temples. Did it in any way help to protect the temple or serve the cause of Hinduism? Personally, he was as much an idol-worshipper as an idol-breaker, remarked Gandhiji, and he put it to his audience that the same held good in respect of them—Hindus and non-Hindus alike—whether they admitted it or not. He would hug an idol and lay down his life to protect it rather than brook any restriction upon his freedom of worship. He had come to help them realize the extent of the madness to which they had stooped. The ruined houses of the Muslims, which he had visited that day, had almost brought tears to his eyes but he had steeled his heart. Bihar, the famous land of Buddha, was surely capable of such rising that it could radiate its effulgence over the rest of India. Only unadulterated non-violence could raise it to that status.

Gandhiji believed that the departure of Muslims from the straight path of non-violence which they had allowed themselves during the 1942 movement, was very probably responsible for their recent aberration. He gave instances of the spirit of general lawlessness which had seized them. They travelled without tickets, they pulled chains in trains or in senseless vindictiveness, burnt zamindars' crops or belongings, and so on. The best way to change the economic and social systems was possible only through the royal road of self-suffering. Any departure from it would result only in changing the form of evil without eradicating it.

The next day, Gandhiji visited the ruined village of Parsa. On the way, his car was stopped at the village of Sipara by the villagers who presented him with a purse. On opening it, Gandhiji found among the coins the following repentance letter signed by the villagers of Sipara:

Please forgive us our great sin. We feel ashamed for the loss of life and property which our Muslim brethren have suffered at our hands. As a token of repentance and expiation for our sin, we present you this purse for the relief of the Muslim victims of the disturbances. We again beg your pardon and assure you that such a thing will never happen again.

In the course of his prayer address at Abdullah Chak that evening, Gandhiji remarked that he wanted every Indian to feel that he had a share in every evil deed committed anywhere in India, no matter by whom and against whom, and that upon all lay the burden of undoing it.

At Khusrupur, Gandhiji remarked that the country is left with only two choices: either tit for tat or unadulterated non-violence. Champaran Satyagraha of 1917 was an education in the latter. Nostalgically, he recalled his first Satyagraha struggle in India in Champaran in 1917; how Rajendra Babu, Brijkishore Babu, Dharni Babu, Gorakh Babu and other leaders of Bihar renounced lucrative careers and a life of comfort and ease to turn themselves into humble servants of humanity, messing in a common kitchen, washing their own clothes and dishes and performing other humble chores, instead of getting them done by servants. Would they rise to the occasion and revive the tradition of Champaran once again?

The non-violent fight which he had launched against injustice and oppression in Champaran had sent new life pulsating throughout

India. History would repeat itself if Biharis played their part. Gandhiji admitted that it was comparatively easy to fight the British but difficult to conquer one's own weaknesses.

But the recent Bihar happenings had forced him to reach to the conclusion that their non-violence was practised by the weak. In the crisis that lay ahead, such non-violence would be of no avail. Only the non-violence of the strong could prove effective. If the way of non-violence of the strong appealed to their head and heart, as a first step towards it they had to come forward and do reparation for the injury of their Muslim brethren, as a token of their sincere repentance. If, on the other hand, they did not honestly believe in it and imagined that the way of violence was the proper answer to the challenge of the times, they should say so frankly and truthfully. "I would not be hurt by the truth but I would prefer not to live to see the failure of the method of non-violence."

As a result of his experience during three short visits which he had paid to the neighbouring villages, Gandhiji came to the conclusion that things had so far settled down, that the refugees could now safely go back to their original homes, if they could overcome the horror of what had happened. The villagers had swarmed to hear him and listened to his severe castigation and exhortations to repentance with rapt attention. The healthy competition among the people in rags in contributing their coppers to the fund for the relief of the riot-affected Muslims was in itself a reassuring sign.

* * *

Khan Abdul Ghaffar Khan had been prevailed upon to visit Bihar. There is nothing more dramatic in recent history than the conversion of this dour Pathan Chieftain to the doctrine of non-violence and the rise of the Khudai Khidmatgar Movement (Servants of God Movement) in pursuance of that ideal under his leadership, among a people reputed to be the most warlike in the world, with "lawlessness of centuries" running in their blood. He became a tower of strength to all in Bihar, standing four-square to every storm. His firmness and unwavering faith in non-violence and human nature shone like a beacon in the tempestuous darkness of the night.

He did not mince words. Such was the respect in which he was held by all, by virtue of his selfless service, sincerity and moral fervour that he could speak with authority to Hindus and Muslims alike. The Bihar Ministers listened with respect to his straight-from-the-shoulder talk; he had fully earned the right. Never for a moment did his faith falter. Above the pandemonium of insanity, his voice rose calm and clear.

"India, today, seems an inferno of madness and my heart weeps to see our homes set on fire by ourselves," he remarked at a joint gathering of Hindus, Muslims and Sikhs, held in Gurudwara Har Mandir, the birth-place of Sikh Guru Govind Singh, in Patna. "I find today darkness reigning over India."

But it was going to be no plain sailing for Gandhiji. It was a rocky path. A meeting that he had with the local Congressmen at Bir served powerfully to remind him of it.

The room was full to capacity. Shah Uzair Munimi, the Muslim District Congress President, had finished his description of the devastation in the Patna district. Gandhiji asked if they had thought what was to be done next. Shah Uzair replied that if they could get even a few honest men, everything could be set right. That gave Gandhiji his cue. He gave to the Congressmen assembled there a most vigorous shaking. He had vowed to "Do or Die" in Bihar. He would not rest nor let others rest; he would wander all over and ask the skeletons lying about how all that had happened. There was such a fire raging in him, he said, that he would know no peace till he had found the reply to the challenge that the recent happenings had flung in their face.

He recalled how a similar restlessness had seized him at the time of Noakhali. The fire in him would not let him rest; he had started walking barefoot from village to village. It seemed to him that in Bihar he might also have to undergo the same ordeal.

On his way to the prayer ground that evening, Gandhiji visited Andari and Gorraiakhari villages. Andari had a population of 462 Hindus and 168 Muslims before the riot. Muslims from the surrounding villages congregated in Andari. When a mob attacked Andari, the Muslims started defending themselves with the courage of despair. They were confident that with a gun and a pistol at their disposal, they could ward off any attack. Some of them, it was stated, even killed their womenfolk with their own hands to prevent their falling into the hands of the mob. But the ammunition ran short. Thereupon, the mob in their mad fury swept before them the handful of defenders. When Gandhiji visited the village, not a single Muslim was there.

Gandhiji received a repentance letter:

Revered Bapu,

At your sacred feet, we of Andari and the surrounding villages declare with God as witness that we are extremely sorry for what has happened. The occasion which has brought you here and which has caused you so much pain is a matter of shame for us. We swear before you that we of Andari and the surrounding villages will henceforth regard the Muslims as our blood-brothers, as we used to before the unfortunate occurrence. For the sin we have committed we beg your and God's pardon.

People of Andari and surrounding villages

The letter was signed by 60 people.

The sight at Gorraiakhari was nerve shaking. Situated on an elevation overlooking green fields below, it must have been a lovely little village. It had a population of 400 Muslims and 20 Hindus. Even the Government report said that out of this, 119 Muslims had been killed. The houses were all in ruins, and spoke of the vandalism of the riotous mob. The village was completely deserted. It was almost impossible to get into any of the houses as the entrances were all blocked by debris. The atmosphere bore the stench of decaying bodies. Gandhiji moved through the lanes of the dead with a heavy heart.

Grief becomes a luxury when atonement calls for appropriate deeds. In his post-prayer address, Gandhiji asked the audience to try their best to get the destroyed villages in their neighbourhood rehabilitated. They should beg the Muslims to forget the past and entreat them, with full guarantee of safety and protection, to come back.

Gandhiji returned to Masaurhi on 20th March. He had seen such wreckage, he remarked in his post-prayer speech, as he dared not try to describe for fear of bursting into tears. It was a sad commentary on them that even months after the carnage the debris had not yet been removed and belongings were being stolen every day from the deserted Muslim houses. It was their duty to rebuild what they had destroyed.

* * *

While Gandhiji was thus preoccupied, disquieting news began to come in from the Punjab and Noakhali. The Muslim League had launched a "Direct Action" campaign. The Hindus, on their part, had decided to observe a "Punjab Day" in Bihar as a protest. A similar report about a proposal by the League to observe a "Pakistan Day" had come from Noakhali. As a result, the Hindus were feeling nervous. Gandhiji appealed to both sides to give up the idea. The Bengal Chief Minister had asked him to visit Bihar. If, therefore, he wanted him to carry on his work in Bihar uninterrupted, Gandhiji said, he should ban the proposed observance of "Pakistan Day" in Noakhali.

The next day, Gandhiji shifted his camp to Hasadiha, where there was a meeting with the village representatives. They told him that people felt that only when the looted property of the Hindus in Noakhali was returned, could the Muslim looted property be returned in Bihar. Gandhiji was further told that withdrawal of cases against the accused was necessary for the reunion of hearts. Again, it was Noakhali in the reverse. It burnt Gandhiji through and through. Did they mean to say, he asked, that if Muslims turned goondas, Hindus also should do so? Shameful things had happened in Noakhali, but the way they were said to have butchered children and even old women in Bihar, and the scale on which they had done it, had far eclipsed Noakhali. Had Indian humanity sunk so low? Did they want to reduce religion to a competition in bestiality?

The evening prayer was held at Ghorhuan, a small village with a population of 200 Hindus and 80 Muslims. Fresh sights of destruction, where men, women and children had been brutally done to death, once more shook Gandhiji deeply.

He paid a glowing tribute to those brave men and women, who had risked the wrath of the violent mobs to save Muslim lives and Muslim property during the mad upheaval. He congratulated them though he knew they did not want any congratulations. About 50 persons, who were wanted in connection with the riot cases, had surrendered on the day after his arrival at Masaurhi. Gandhiji hoped that many others, who had taken part in the riot, would follow, make a clean breast of what they had done, and take whatever punishment might be meted out to them.

While returning to Patna the following morning, Gandhiji met a batch of Muslim women refugees in the village Pipalwan. Always sensitive to the sufferings of the weak and the oppressed, he was greatly moved by their tales of woe. Many of them had lost their husbands, children and dear ones. He told them that they should not bear ill-will against the evildoers, nor seek revenge. That would be true bravery.

Summing up his impressions of the six days' tour of the affected area, Gandhiji observed that while the vestiges of terrible happenings which he had seen were such as to make a man almost despair of humanity, he had also seen unmistakable signs of the dawn of a new era. The villagers were not only genuinely penitent over what had happened but were also willing to atone for the past. They had contributed their humble mite liberally for the relief of the Muslims. Again and again they had stopped his car on the way to present him with purses. They had addressed him letters expressing their readiness and willingness to help in the rehabilitation of the Muslims. In a number of places Muslims themselves had come and told him that the absence of incidents in those places was due to the bravery of the local Hindus. Many of those who were wanted in connection with the riots had come and surrendered to the authorities. He hoped many more would come forward and acknowledge their guilt.

But the whole body politic of India was in a desperate strait. No sooner was the symptom allayed in one place, than the disease broke out in a more virulent form in another. Sardar Patel had written to Gandhiji that a sort of peace seemed to have been established in the Punjab through military measures. Gandhiji saw no peace in that stillness of the grave. His penetrating eyes saw beneath and beyond the superficial and the immediate. If the Punjab was quietened down by the use of superior force, the seed of further quarrel and bitterness between the Hindus and the Muslims would be sown for all time. From the information that had reached him, the people in the Punjab were silently preparing for open and deadlier fights. If that went on, he warned prophetically, *after a certain stage even the military would find it impossible to control the situation.* True peace would come only when at least one side, if not both, adopted the true bravery that is non-violence.

During the week which was destined to be practically his last in the province, Gandhiji put final touches to the scheme for rehabilitation which the Government had prepared in consultation with him. He had tackled a similar situation in Noakhali. His plan was based on an unshakeable faith in the fundamental goodness of humanity. It was this latent fund of goodness in the human heart which he wanted to release by evoking true repentance in the hearts of the wrongdoers, and courage and forgiveness in those of the victims. For this he needed to establish his bona fides with both.

In Noakhali, the Hindus had faith in him while the attitude of the Muslims, in the bulk, was unfriendly. That he had not been able to convince the Muslims of his sincerity in spite of a lifetime of service, he characteristically attributed to some shortcoming within himself. The remedy, he argued, lay in still greater self-purification. For that he needed God's grace. Such was the inner urge he felt in that supreme hour to throw himself entirely on God that, sending away all his old associates, he set forth on a village-to-village tour on foot in the devastated area, until true heart-unity was established between the two communities. As he trekked barefoot through villages that had been the scene of devastation, through gloomy forest depths and amongst people who had been taught to regard him as their worst enemy, he gave them a chance of seeing him at close quarters and judging for themselves whether he was their enemy or their friend. More and more Muslims came to his prayer meetings. He reminded them of the noble teachings of their religion and how they had dealt it a cowardly blow and degraded themselves by behaving like beasts in respect of the minority domiciled in their midst.

In Bihar, the picture was reversed. It was the Muslims who had been the sufferers. He gave them the same message of courage and reliance on God, as he had given to the Hindu riot victims in Noakhali.' He knew that the safety of the minority lay only in the re-establishment of the unity of heart between Hindus and Muslims —not in arms, not in the Muslim Police. These were remedies born of despair, likely to only aggravate the disease.

With the Hindus of Bihar, Gandhiji had a tremendous advantage. At places, the Hindus went to the refugee camps as suggested by him, brought back the Muslims and fed them at their own expense. Crowds vied with one another in contributing to the Muslim relief fund. There was a distinct improvement in the atmosphere in the villages.

Before Gandhiji finally left Bihar, he had lain down the lines along which rehabilitation should work. He had hoped to return and complete what remained. He was sure that if the poison could be effectively neutralized anywhere in India, its influence would spread. But God had willed it otherwise. He could never settle down in Bihar.

9

"ONE-MAN BOUNDARY FORCE"

A tumult raged within Gandhiji during the later part of June and through July, while he was in the capital.

Bihar called him. So did Noakhali. When in the last week of May he left Patna, he had expected to return to Bihar within a week. But events had since happened in such quick succession that a generation seemed to be packed into a month. The Punjab also seemed to call him. Storm-clouds were gathering in that key province. Where lay his duty?

In the last week of July, the Partition Council, fearful of the repercussions the Boundary Commission's awards might have on areas affected by them, decided to set up a Boundary Force with a nucleus of "some fifty thousand officers and men, mainly composed of mixed units not yet partitioned and containing a high proportion of British officers" in the Punjab partition areas. This probably was "the largest military force ever collected in any one area of a country for the maintenance of law and order in peace-time".

His place in the circumstances, Gandhiji felt, was not in the capital but with the men of "the tattered battalion which fights till it dies". In the words of John Masefield,

Theirs be the music, the colour, the glory, the gold;

Mine be a handful of ashes, a mouthful of mould.

Of the maimed, of the halt and the blind in the rain and the cold.

Gandhiji bypassed Delhi on his way back from Kashmir as he journeyed straight from Lahore to Patna. Thence he would go to

Noakhali via Calcutta. Nobody tried to dissuade him this time. They all realized that given the way he felt about Partition and the coming 15th August celebrations, he would be out of place in the midst of the official rejoicing at the capital on Independence Day.

If fear and panic are infectious, so is courage, particularly when its facet is that of non-violence. Gandhiji's utterances in Kashmir and elsewhere had travelled before him and produced a most salutary effect all over the province. When only a week earlier, on his way to Kashmir, he had passed through Amritsar, some youngsters had staged a black flag demonstration at the railway station with shouts of "Gandhi, go back." Now, as the train pulled in, thousands of people were seen lined up on the platform in front of his compartment in perfect order. They asked for his bag which they said they would send afterwards stuffed with collections for the Harijan fund. They were profuse in their apologies for the unseemly scene on the previous occasion. "It was an egregious mistake on our part. We did not know. Your four days' visit to our province has transformed the whole atmosphere. Please, forgive us."

Gandhiji's magnanimous reply was: "Forget the past. Remember the saying, 'Our day dawns from the moment we wake up.' Let us all wake up now."

* * *

Calcutta had never really been peaceful since the Great Calcutta Killing of August 1946. Bitter memories of the "Direct Action" Day and what the Hindus had suffered under the Muslim League rule were rankling in people's hearts. Communal frenzy had continued to boil and simmer beneath the surface. Murder, arson and loot, the use of fire-arms and the throwing of bombs and acid bulbs became a regular feature of life in the city. Organized life in some parts of the city had almost been paralyzed. Areas had been divided into "Hindu" and "Muslim". Hindus could not walk even in broad daylight through Muslim quarters and vice versa. On top of all this, as a result of the freedom given to government servants under the Partition Plan to opt for either Dominion, almost all Muslim officers and police had opted for Pakistan and Hindus had taken their places. The Muslims were now panic-stricken.

After his arrival at Sodepur Ashram, Mohammad Usman, the Muslim League leader and an ex-Mayor of Calcutta, came to Gandhiji. They complained that since the Muslims in the services had almost all been transferred to East Bengal, the Hindus of West Bengal thought that they could now do whatever they liked "to get even with the Muslims"; Gandhiji alone could save the Muslims of Calcutta. Could he not stay in Calcutta for a while, "to throw a pot of water", as the saying went, on the fire that was raging in the city?

Gandhiji devoted the whole of his prayer address that evening to the situation in Calcutta. He had been coming across with the tales of woe of the Muslims of Calcutta the whole day. He was not going to hold an inquiry into what had been done under the League ministry. He was more concerned with what his friend Dr Ghosh's ministry was doing. Was it true that the Muslims of Calcutta were living in terror? If so, it was a severe reflection on the Congress ministry. He could never accept the plea, he said, that all that was happening in Calcutta was the work of hooligans. "The Government must hold itself responsible also for the acts of the so-called goondas."

The next day, Mohammad Usman came again accompanied by a large Muslim deputation. They entreated Gandhiji to stay on in Calcutta even if it were only for two more days. "We, Muslims, have as much claim upon you as the Hindus."

Gandhiji clarified: "I am willing, but then you will have to guarantee the peace of Noakhali. If I do not go to Noakhali before the 15th on the strength of your guarantee, and things go wrong there, my life will become forfeit; you will have to face a fast unto death on my part."

Mohammad Usman and the Muslim friends were taken aback by this. The responsibility was great and the risk was heavy. They hesitated but ultimately gave the required guarantee on the Muslim League's behalf. They promised to dispatch wires to the local League leaders in Noakhali. To reinforce the telegrams they undertook to send emissaries to help maintain the peace in Noakhali.

Gandhiji told them that though he was anxious to reach Noakhali as soon as possible, in deference to their wishes he could postpone going from the 11th to the 13th August.

Announcing the decision at the prayer meeting, he remarked that it was unthinkable that the majority could, for one moment, be permitted to coerce the minority. He had been told that, now that the Congress ministry was in power, the Hindu police and officers had become partial, and were doing what the Muslim police and officers were alleged to have done before. He was loath to believe it.

At this stage, Shaheed Suhrawardy entered upon the scene. He was at Karachi. Upon learning that Gandhiji was on his way to Noakhali, he rushed to Calcutta. It would be incongruous on his part to leave Calcutta while the city was burning, he told Gandhiji in an hour and a half's talk extending nearly to midnight. He should prolong his stay in the city until real peace was restored. Gandhiji replied that he was willing to do so if Suhrawardy was prepared to work in association with him for restoring peace. He suggested that they should both live together under the same roof in the disturbed parts, *unprotected by the police or the military*, together meet the people, argue with them and tell them that now that partition had taken place by mutual agreement, there was no longer any reason why the parties should continue to quarrel. If Suhrawardy accepted the offer, he on his part would postpone his going to Noakhali and remain in Calcutta as long as it was necessary.

But the proposal was of too serious a nature for an immediate reply. Gandhiji asked him to take his time, and then communicate to him his decision.

Shaheed Suhrawardy, in August, 1947, after his dethronement in the Council of the Muslim League, was a different man from the power-conscious Chief Minister of Bengal. Only three months back he had turned down an almost identical offer by Gandhiji as a "mad offer".

The next day Mohammad Usman brought Shaheed's reply accepting without reservation Gandhiji's proposal. Accordingly, Gandhiji announced that he had decided to prolong his stay in Calcutta indefinitely to see what Shaheed Suhrawardy and he could do by working together to achieve real communal peace in the city. He had been warned, he remarked, that Suhrawardy was not to be relied upon. But had not the same been said about himself as well? He would trust, as he expected to be trusted. Both he and Suhrawardy would live under the same roof. They would have no secrets from each other. They would meet all visitors together. People should have the courage to speak out the truth in every circumstance—even in the presence of those against whom charges had to be proffered.

* * *

It was Gandhiji's unvarying practice on the eve of all important decisions to intimate them to his close associates by writing personal letters. The day's post included nearly a dozen such letters, all written in his own hand. The work continued non-stop till half past one. He had sent word to Suhrawardy that he would be starting for his new residence in Beliaghata exactly at 2.30 in the afternoon and Shaheed should arrive in time to accompany him. As Shaheed did not turn up, Gandhiji with his never failing punctuality started for Beliaghata according to plan.

Hydari Mansion, an old abandoned Muslim house in an indescribably filthy locality, had hastily been cleaned up for Gandhiji's residence. It was a ramshackle building open on all sides to the crowds. There was only one latrine and it was used indiscriminately by hundreds of people, including the police on duty and the visitors. Owing to the rains, there was mud and slush. It stank. To drown the stink, bleaching powder was sprinkled liberally all over the place, which made one's head reel.

An excited crowd of young men stood at the gate as Gandhiji's car arrived. They shouted: "Why have you come here? You did not come when we were in trouble. Now that the Muslims have complained, all this fuss is being made over it. Why did you not go to places from where the Hindus have fled?"

A little while later, Suhrawardy's car arrived. The angry crowd surrounded it. The situation threatened to take an ugly turn. Gandhiji sent some of his men to tell the demonstrators to send in their representatives to meet him. This was done. The rest of the demonstrators thereupon calmed down and allowed Suhrawardy to go in. The demonstration was still going on when Horace Alexander, who had been asked by Gandhiji to come and stay with him at Beliaghata, arrived.

Some young men tried to climb up to the window of Gandhiji's room. Members of his party begged them to desist. It was no use. Horace began to shut the windows. Almost immediately stones were thrown and glass was flying in all directions.

Presently, the representatives of the demonstrators were ushered in to meet Gandhiji. One of them began: "Last year, when 'Direct Action' was launched on the Hindus you did not come to our rescue. Now that there has been just a little trouble in the Muslim quarters, you have come running to their succour. We don't want you here."

Gandhiji replied: "Much water has flown under the bridge since August, 1946. What the Muslims did then was utterly wrong. But what is the use of avenging the year 1946 in 1947? I was on my way to Noakhali where your own kith and kin desired my presence. But I now see that I shall have to serve Noakhali only from here. You must understand that I have come here to serve Hindus, Muslims and all alike. Those who are indulging in brutalities are bringing disgrace upon themselves and the religion they represent. I am going to put myself under your protection. You are welcome to turn against me or play the opposite role if you so choose. I have nearly reached the end of my life's journey. I don't have much farther to go. But let me tell you that if you again go mad, I will not be a living witness to it. I have given the same ultimatum to the Muslims of Noakhali also; I have earned the right. Why cannot you see that by taking this step I have put the burden of peace in Noakhali on the shoulders of Shaheed Suhrawardy and his friends? This is no small gain."

"We do not want your sermons on ahimsa. You go away from here. We won't allow the Muslims to live here."

"This means that you do not want my services. If you will cooperate with me and allow me to carry on my work, it will enable the Hindus to return and live in all the places from where they have been driven out. On the other hand, it will profit you nothing to remember old wrongs and nurse old enmities."

An 18-year-old interposed: "History shows that Hindus and Muslims can never be friends. Anyway, ever since I was born I have seen them only fighting each other."

Gandhiji said: "Well, I have seen more of history than anyone of you, and I tell you that I have known Hindu boys who called Muslims 'uncle'. Hindus and Muslims used to participate in each others' festivals and other auspicious occasions. You want to force me to leave this place, but you should know that I have never submitted to force. It is contrary to my nature. You can obstruct my work, even kill me. I won't invoke the help of the police. To make me quit, you have to convince me that I have made a mistake in coming here."

Thus it went on till eight o'clock. At last, Gandhiji said: "I put it to you, young men, how can I, who am a Hindu by birth, a Hindu by creed and a Hindu of Hindus in my way of living, be an 'enemy' of Hindus? Does this not show narrow intolerance on your part?"

His words had a profound effect. Slowly and imperceptibly the opposition began to soften. Still, they were not completely converted. One of them said, "Perhaps we should now go." Gandhiji replied, "Yes, you must go. It is already late. Come again in the morning when you have thought things over."

At 11, Gandhiji went to bed without any food.

The next day—14th August—proved to be as hectic as the previous one. The young men came again and, in Suhrawardy's presence, had a long session with Gandhiji. In the course of the discussion, Gandhiji pointed out to them that united action on the part of Suhrawardy and himself in Beliaghata was only the first step. If and when the Hindus of Beliaghata invited their Muslim neighbours to return, they would next move to a predominantly Muslim area, where they would stay till the Hindus were invited to return and so on till each community had invited its neighbours to return to their former houses all over Calcutta.

This time the young men were completely won over. They undertook to do all within their power to convince their friends to work with Gandhiji for peace and goodwill. Afterwards, one of them said to another: "What a spell-binder this old man is! No matter how heavy the odds, he does not know defeat!"

The evening prayer was held inside the compound of the Hydari Mansion. It was attended by over 10,000 people. In the course of his address, Gandhiji said: "From tomorrow (15th August), we shall be delivered from the bondage of British rule. But from midnight today, India will be partitioned too. While, therefore, tomorrow will be a day of rejoicing, it will be a day of sorrow as well. It will throw a heavy burden of responsibility upon us. Let us pray to God that He may give us strength to bear it worthily. Let all those Muslims who were forced to flee return to their homes. If two millions of Hindus and Muslims are at daggers in Calcutta, with what face can I go to Noakhali and plead the cause of the Hindus with the Muslims there?"

"Where is Suhrawardy?" the gathering shouted.

"He is inside the house," Gandhiji answered. "He has, with my consent, kept himself away from the meeting as he wanted to avoid giving the slightest cause for irritation. But in view of the becoming tolerance which you have shown today, I shall be encouraged to bring him to the meeting from tomorrow onwards."

Realizing that Suhrawardy was not at the prayer meeting, some of the young men decided that this was the moment to attack him. They went shouting for his blood towards the house and stone-throwing began again.

Prayer over, Gandhiji returned to his room and sat down to work. But the uproar continued outside, though the stone-throwing stopped. After a few minutes he beckoned Manu, went with her to the window and began to address the crowd outside. Rapidly the tumult subsided. There was total silence. He rebuked them for their attack on Suhrawardy. If they had agreed to work with him (Gandhiji) that meant also working with Suhrawardy. The two were as one.

"Where is Suhrawardy?" the people asked. They said they would not disperse unless he appeared before them in person.

Gandhiji told them that Shaheed was inside, engaged in breaking the Ramzan fast. He would appear before them presently.

Someone in the crowd made a caustic remark about Suhrawardy's untrustworthiness. Gandhiji answered: "He will not be able to stick with me if he is not sincere; he will drop off before long."

After a time, when he had got them into a mood to listen to Suhrawardy, he beckoned him (Suhrawardy) to his side and stood there in full view of the crowd, resting one hand tactfully on Shaheed's, the other on Manu's shoulder.

Suhrawardy addressed the gathering: "It is Bengal's great good luck that Mahatmaji is in our midst at this hour. Will Bengal realize its high privilege and stop the fratricide?"

One of the crowd: "Are you not responsible for the Great Calcutta Killing?"

Suhrawardy: "Yes, we all are."

"Will you answer my question, please?"

"Yes, it was my responsibility."

This unequivocal, straight and candid confession of his guilt by one who had made arrogance and haughtiness his badge and never known humility, had a profound effect on the crowd. "It was the turning point," Gandhiji afterwards remarked. "It had a cleansing effect. I could sense it."

Just then news began to arrive that a mixed Hindu and Muslim procession estimated to be not less than 5000 had come out on the streets. In one part of the city, it was reported, some Hindus were trying to put up the national flag for the next morning. The Muslims on the other side of the street called out, "Shall we come and help you, brothers?" Their offer was immediately accepted. Remarked Suhrawardy, "Look at the miracle that Mahatmaji has wrought in a single day!"

At night, Suhrawardy took Gandhiji to the Lake for a walk. By the time they returned it was already 10.00.

Once again, it was 11 when he went to bed. But the shouts of *jays* (shouts of acclamation on attaining victory) could be heard throughout the night. The whole city was in a gala mood. Flags, buntings and singing crowds were everywhere in evidence in anticipation of the great day—15th August. Hindus and Muslims were seen intermingling till late in the night in many areas.

At Gandhiji's request, armed guards were withdrawn from his residence and their place was taken by volunteers, Hindus and Muslims in equal number. Gandhiji's Muslim host decorated the house with the national flag on the eve of the transfer of power.

* * *

On Independence Day, Gandhiji woke up at 2 am—an hour earlier than usual. It being the fifth death anniversary of Mahadev Desai also, he observed it, according to his practice on such occasions, by fasting and having a recitation of the whole *Gita*.

The prayer was still in progress when strains of music broke in. A batch of girls, singing Tagore's beautiful songs of freedom, was approaching the house. They came and stopped outside the window of Gandhiji's room. Reverently, they stopped their singing, joined the prayers, afterwards sang again and departed. A little later, another batch of girls came and sang songs likewise and so it continued till dawn—a beautiful beginning to the day, after the tumult of the previous evening.

Men, women and children in their thousands were waiting for his *darshan* as he went out for his morning walk. Eager crowds besieged the mansion the whole day. Every half an hour he had to come out to give *darshan*. The members of the West Bengal cabinet also came for his blessings. Gandhiji said to them: "From today, you have to wear the crown of thorns. Strive ceaselessly to cultivate truth and non-violence. Be humble. Be forbearing. Beware of power; power corrupts. Do not let yourselves be entrapped by its pomp and pageantry. Remember, you are in office to serve the poor in India's villages. May God help you."

Stirring scenes of national rejoicing marked by unique demonstrations of Hindu-Muslim unity were witnessed in Calcutta on 15th August. From early morning, mixed parties of Hindus and Muslims began to go about in trucks to various parts of the city shouting slogans, "*Hindu Muslim ek ho* (Let Hindus and Muslims unite)" and "*Hindu Muslim bhai bhai* (Hindus and Muslims are brothers)". Till late at night vast crowds jammed all thoroughfares, sending up deafening shouts of "*Jay Hind* (Victory to India)". It was as if after the black clouds of a year of madness, the sunshine of sanity and goodwill had suddenly broken through.

But Gandhiji's face betrayed no sign of exuberance.

Nearly 30,000 persons gathered that evening in the prayer ground. Gandhiji congratulated the citizens of Calcutta on account of the unity they had achieved. It saddened him all the more to hear, he said, that madness still raged in Lahore. He felt sure that the noble example of Calcutta, if it was sincere, would affect the Punjab and other parts of India. He warned the people that now that they were free, they were to use their freedom with wise restraint. They had to realize that they were masters of no one but themselves. They dare not compel anyone to do anything against their will.

Following Gandhiji, Suhrawardy addressed the gathering. Until the Hindus went back to their abandoned homes and the Muslims to theirs, he said, they would not think that their work was finished. Some people thought, he continued, that Hindu-Muslim unity could never be achieved, "but by God's will and Mahatmaji's grace, what was considered an impossibility only three or four days ago had miraculously turned into fact." With that, he asked the mixed gathering of Hindus and Muslims to shout "*Jay Hind*" with him, which they did with a deafening roar. A faint, ineffable smile played on Gandhiji's lips as he watched the soul-stirring scene.

At night, Gandhiji made a tour of the city and witnessed scenes of fraternization in various places. Suhrawardy drove the car. At a crowded street corner the people recognized them and hundreds of Muslims instantly surrounded the car. They shouted, "*Mahatma Gandhi zindabad* (Long live Mahatma Gandhi)." Some sprinkled rose water and scent over them.

Gandhiji observed the day by fasting and spinning extra. Suhrawardy fasted with him.

* * *

As Gandhiji went out for his usual walk the next morning, a vast crowd lined his route. He utilized their presence to impress upon them the necessity of observing voluntary restraint and discipline on festive occasions and requested them to spare him the ordeal of shouting. The shouting died out at once.

The crowds had made the precincts of Gandhiji's residence filthy by spitting all around. To give them a lesson in cleanliness, he began to go out for his walks barefoot. There was an immediate improvement.

The prayer meeting on the 16th August was attended by nearly 50,000 people. On the following day, it was attended by over 100,000 people. As Gandhiji viewed the surging mass delirious with enthusiasm, he again wondered how far their enthusiasm was genuine and what the depth of their feeling really was. Voicing a sudden misgiving within him, he said: "Let us all thank God for His abundant mercy. But let us not forget that there are isolated spots in Calcutta, where all is not well. I have heard that in one place the Hindus are not prepared to welcome back the Muslim residents who were obliged to leave their homes."

Suhrawardy announced that Muslims had invited their Hindu brethren to participate in the Id reunion. He had also been informed that many Hindus had expressed their intention to send food to the mosques for their Muslim brethren to break their fast. Referring to the large attendance of Hindus and Muslims at the meeting, Suhrawardy said that no one could dream a few days ago that such a big meeting of both the communities could be held in Calcutta or that Hindus could pass through localities predominantly inhabited by Muslims without being harmed and vice versa.

Proceeding, Suhrawardy narrated how when he went to the Park Circus area with the objective of forming reception committees to welcome Hindus back to their abandoned homes with garlands, he found that they were already going to their deserted houses without waiting for the formation of the committees and fraternizing with the Muslims, and this in an area where, till a few days back, even Sikh drivers dared not ply their taxis. This miracle had been achieved, Suhrawardy repeated, "by the grace of God and through Mahatmaji's grace." Continuing, he remarked amidst laughter that they all knew he did not say all this before. The mistake they had committed was now a thing of the past.

"Why did I run to Mahatmaji?" Suhrawardy resumed. "It was because I felt that if the trouble started here, it would spread to other parts of India and if it was checked here, there would be peace elsewhere. With this end in view I approached Mahatmaji and through God's grace it seems that the hatchet has been buried for ever." With a "*Jay Hind*", he concluded his speech.

Could this be the same Suhrawardy who had been responsible for the Great Calcutta Killing?—people wondered.

But Gandhiji's "sixth sense" saw beneath the surface something more than met the eye.

Gandhiji to Mirabehn   18th August, 1947
Hindu-Muslim unity seems to be too sudden to be true. Time will show.

The prayer meeting that evening was attended by not less than half a million. Muslims were present in unusually large numbers. It was an inspiring spectacle against the background of communal fratricide in other parts of the country to find the Hindus and Muslims of Calcutta standing shoulder to shoulder. They cheered Gandhiji as he stood up with folded hands to acknowledge their greetings and wished them a happy Id.

Gandhiji was delighted to receive a telephone message from Bihar saying that the Calcutta miracle was having a profound effect on Bihar, too.

In a women's meeting on 21st August, he asked all Hindu women to go among their Muslim sisters, befriend them and render them every service they were capable of. By way of self-purification, they had to root out the last trace of untouchability from their hearts. He had always maintained that the Hindu-Muslim question was only a projection of the blemish of untouchability which Hinduism had harboured in its soul.

Nearly 700,000 people attended the prayer meeting which was held each day in a different part of the city. Gandhiji felt he could now proceed to Noakhali.

* * *

People have often wondered what enabled Gandhiji to command and retain the loyalty, devotion and sacrifice of so many diverse elements and hold them prisoners of his love. How did he manage to reconcile and harmonize such a vast medley of conflicting temperaments and interests to build up the power of non-violence? It was due to the reckless abandon with which he burnt the candle at both ends to light the path of those who needed his guidance; the measure of his concern for and identification with those who had dedicated themselves to the cause; his mellowed wisdom; the concentrated attention he gave to every detail of constructive work which provided the organization and drive behind his non-violent mass upheavals; and the originality which he brought to bear upon any problem he touched.

* * *

The events of Calcutta had by now begun to radiate their influence in other parts of the country besides Bihar. On 24th August, the

Muslim League Party in the Constituent Assembly of the Indian Union passed a resolution expressing "its deep sense of appreciation of the services rendered by Mahatma Gandhi to the cause of restoration of peace and goodwill between the communities in Calcutta and saving hundreds of innocent lives and property from destruction. By his ceaseless efforts in the cause of maintenance of peace, he has shown breadth of vision and large-heartedness."

What a pity that this realization of Gandhiji's "breadth of vision" and "large-heartedness" came only after India had been cut into two and so much innocent blood had been shed!

In an article titled "Miracle or Accident?" in *Harijan*, Gandhiji wrote:

> The joy of fraternization is leaping up from hour to hour. Is this to be called a miracle or an accident? This sudden upheaval is not the work of one or two men. We are toys in the hands of God. He makes us dance to His tune. I only ask whether the dream of my youth is to be realized in the evening of my life.
>
> We have drunk the poison of mutual hatred and so this nectar of fraternization tastes all the sweeter and the sweetness should never wear out.

Wrote Lord Mountbatten to Gandhiji: "In the Punjab, we have 55,000 soldiers and large-scale rioting on our hands. In Bengal, our forces consist of one man, and there is no rioting. As a serving officer, as well as an administrator, may I be allowed to pay my tribute to the One-Man Boundary Force, not forgetting his Second in Command, Mr Suhrawardy?"

10

CRUMBLING HEAVENS

What Gandhiji had feared all along, and prophesied again and again to unheeding ears, happened at last. The heavens began to crumble in the Punjab. On the 17th August, he received the following wire in Calcutta:

A terrible massacre of the Hindus has been in progress in Lahore city, surpassing Rawalpindi. Hundreds of dead are lying strewn on the roads. The greater part of the city is in flames. Water supply in Hindu residential quarters has been cut off. The trapped Hindus, who tried to escape, were shot down by the military. More than 300 Hindus were burnt alive. The Hindus are without food and water. They are threatened with destruction. Do something immediately. Your presence in Lahore is necessary.

Jawaharlal Nehru had gone on a two-day visit to the affected areas. On his return to Delhi he wired to Gandhiji telling him that the Punjab needed his "healing presence".

Gandhiji replied from Calcutta: "I have got stuck here. Noakhali demands my presence. Bihar, too, will take a few days. Under the circumstances I do not know when I shall be able to go to the Punjab. You will guide me."

A deputation of the Punjabis in Calcutta saw Gandhiji.

Gandhiji to Nehru   24th August, 1947

Punjabis in Calcutta have been pressing me to go to the Punjab at once. They tell me terrible tales. Thousands have been killed! A few thousand girls have been kidnapped! Hindus cannot live in the Pakistan area, nor Muslims in the other portion. Add to this the information that the two wings of the army took sides and wrought havoc. Can any of this be true!

When do you think I should go to the Punjab, if at all? I still have work in Calcutta, then in Noakhali and Bihar. But everything can be laid aside to go to the Punjab if it is necessary.

Nehru had, in the meantime, gone on his second visit to the East Punjab. Immediately on his return, he wrote:

On both sides of the border in the Punjab people are affected and mass migrations are taking place on a vast scale.

There has been widespread killing on both sides and large numbers of refugees have been massacred. In East Punjab probably the Sikhs have indulged in killing more than anyone else. Worse than the killing have been the horrible outrages on women on both sides.

It is said and rightly that Lahore and Amritsar are quiet. The fact is that there are not many people left there to be killed. That is to say that Lahore has become almost entirely a Muslim city and Amritsar a Hindu-Sikh city.

More and more, both in the East and West Punjab, habitually lawless elements are coming to the front and they are not prepared to listen to the leaders.

* * *

Disquieting news had, in the meantime, reached Sardar Patel from the Wah camp where Gandhiji had left Sushila on his return journey from Kashmir in the first week of August. At first all went well. The refugees were very much heartened. But nervousness returned as soon as Gandhiji's back was turned. "The old man has played us a trick! How clever of him!" remarked one refugee to another. "This girl! How can she protect us?" rejoined another.

Sushila afterwards recorded:

I stayed there, fully convinced that it was wrong for the Hindus and Sikhs to flee from Pakistan. They had inhabited the land for generations and were entitled to live there. If Indians could fight for their rights in South Africa, were they to relinquish their homes in Pakistan?

I placed my ideas before the refugees. Some appreciated them, some were resentful. They were not prepared to live a life of hostages, they said. They would rather be beggars in India than big landlords in Pakistan, where even the honour of their womenfolk was not safe. I tried to impress upon them that the right thing for us to do would be to die in defence of our honour rather than be bullied out.

Then trouble started again. The East Punjab was reported to be avenging Rawalpindi and the whole of the West Punjab flared up to avenge the happenings in the East Punjab. Several victims of communal fury from places around began to pour into the camp hospital. One of them was a young girl of about 17—the sole survivor of a group of 74 women, who had jumped into a well to save their honour. Her father, Sardar Pratap Singh had come to join the camp earlier. He and his companions had offered armed resistance to the Muslim mobs who had attacked their village. For three days they held the attackers at bay. When at last their ammunition was exhausted, they had to surrender. Several of them, including their leader, were wounded, some others had died. The survivors were told that they would immediately be converted to Islam. They asked for reprieve till the next day.

Next morning the hooligans were ready with their scissors to cut off their hair and shave their beards as a symbol of their conversion to Islam. Some among the mob were loudly discussing among themselves as to who was going to have a particular woman to himself. The women heard this. They were ordered to come out to be converted. An elderly sister, speaking for the rest answered that they wanted leave to say their prayers for the last time before they surrendered and drink the water from the well, which had recently been constructed. The request was granted. Thereupon, 74 women and girls entered the compound in which the well was located. They had their ceremonial bath and then began saying their prayers. Their Muslim captors impatiently shouted to them to hurry up. The leader of the women shouted back, "Come if you dare. You will never touch us alive." And with that she jumped into the well followed by the rest.

This act of heroic self-sacrifice so touched the gangsters that they stood rooted to the spot, and with bowed heads departed one after another, leaving untouched the men and the children whom they had assembled for conversion. The Sikhs then entered the compound and brought out the bodies of the women who had jumped into the well. All except Sardar Pratap Singh's daughter were dead. At night, they were attacked by another Muslim mob but a military patrol came to their rescue and escorted them to the Wah camp.

There was a cement factory next door to the camp. It was said to be one of the biggest in the world. I went to visit it. At the end of the visit the factory doctor invited me to his house. He was a Bengali. There was a lovely two-year-old blonde playing in the house. The doctor explained to me that the child was their adopted daughter. She was a Punjabi. The mother had died in the hospital after childbirth and the father had not cared to claim the child. So the doctor and his wife had adopted her and they simply adored her. Suddenly, the doctor's voice became husky: "For the last one week I am constantly haunted by the fear that when I return home, I may not find her there. They will either kill or kidnap her." "Surely, you are unnecessarily anxious," I protested. "No one will touch a child like this and then there are very good security measures in this factory." "Yes," replied the doctor. "But two days ago a Hindu was murdered while passing with his cement cart in front of my house. He was a factory hand. The assassin pushed the dagger into him from behind. The place was full of people. Not one tried to stop him. The assailant escaped and is probably still there. Can't you help send away my wife and child to a place of safety?" There was a note of entreaty in his voice. I was deeply moved. The thought that any one could kill an innocent little child like her made me feel sick. I promised to make arrangements for sending away his wife and child to India as early as possible.

Two days later, I informed the doctor that he could send away his wife and child on the following day, as all necessary arrangements had been made. His face lit up. His wife was a little uneasy at the thought of leaving her husband behind. The doctor turned round to me, "You should also go away with them. This place has become most unsafe."

I thanked him for his kind thought and explained to him that I could not go away. I had to be at my post of duty where Gandhiji had left me. He insisted that I must not expose myself to such grave danger. I must go. "No, I cannot. Please don't worry about me. So long as my time is not up, I shall be safe anywhere and when my time is up, there will be safety for me nowhere." Something in my words and manner must have touched him. He stood up with a new look on his face. "Thank you for the arrangements you have made for my family. But I am not sending them away. If this place is safe for you, it is safe enough for them." There were tears in his eyes. My heart overflowed with gratitude to God and Bapu. I said to myself, "Bapu has put the seed of a little faith and courage in the hearts of insignificant beings like us, which in its turn can inspire similar feeling in other breasts."

By the time I was to leave the Wah camp according to the original programme, life had become most uncertain there. More refugees started pouring in. They were attacked on the way and many of them, including women and children, arrived in a terrible condition. Then, one fine morning (after 15th August), the mixed guard for the camp was replaced by a Pakistani guard. It was reported that he had been overheard telling some local Muslims that they could now attack the camp with impunity. My faith was shaken. No longer could I tell refugees in the camp that they must not think of leaving Pakistan. There were stories about the partisan behaviour of the police and the military and a young Muslim officer of nationalistic views told me that there was much truth in them. I had to acknowledge defeat and write to responsible quarters in the Indian Union pleading for speedy evacuation of the Wah camp.

In the last week of August, Sardar Patel received the following report from Sushila: "We are completely cut off. No post comes or leaves this place. People here are living in hourly fear of certain death. I am trying my best to keep up their morale. They won't allow me to leave this place. It is some consolation that my presence here gives them courage."

In sending to Gandhiji Sushila's report, Sardar Patel wrote to him: "I was very concerned at your leaving Sushila behind. Today a special military man has come with a letter from her. I send it to you."

Gandhiji's reply to Sardar showed how exacting his love could be with respect to those who had identified themselves with him and towards whom he was supposed to be *partial*:

> I had left Sushila literally in the jaws of death. Now she will return only when the Wah refugees feel at ease or perish with them. It was only from your letter that I learnt where she is at present. There was a letter from her from Wah soon after I had left. But there was nothing after that. I was, therefore, wondering.

Sardar Patel to Gandhiji   27th August, 1947

> Rajkumari (Amrit Kaur) had accompanied Lady Mountbatten on a three-day tour of the Punjab. She has brought a terrible report. She met Sushila too. I had asked Lady Mountbatten to bring her back with her. Accordingly, Sushila had got ready. But the people in the camp began to weep and wail. She is, therefore, staying on there. This camp is not in danger. We have now made arrangements for some more supply of food, too. She is keeping quite fit. So there is nothing to worry. The rest, of course, is in God's hands.

* * *

Ever since his departure from Noakhali in the first week of March, 1947, Gandhiji had maintained constant touch with his co-workers in Noakhali. To him, Noakhali and Bihar still held the key to India's future. That was why he was so anxious to get back there as early as possible. In one of his letters to me he wrote: "It fills me with joy to read the accounts of your work. I would like to fly to you. But Kashmir calls me. After the Kashmir visit, I plan to come to Noakhali via Bihar."

At the same time we began to feel more and more the need for guidance by Gandhiji. It was, therefore, decided that two of us, Charu Chowdhury and I, should meet Gandhiji at Calcutta, put before him our point of view and persuade him not to abandon his Noakhali visit.

To see the old familiar face and hear the familiar voice after six months or more was an overwhelming experience.

After a discussion with us, Gandhiji announced that he would be leaving for Noakhali on the 2nd September.

On the previous evening, He, who keeps watch when man's vision fails, gave the warning signal.

Charu and I had gone out to the city on business. When we returned to Hydari Mansion, it was past 10. We had expected to find everybody asleep. Instead, we found the building in a blaze of light. Some youngsters at the gate tried to stop our car with "Who are you —Hindu or Muslim?"

We came out of the car. We brushed them aside and went in. Crowds were all over the place. Some rowdies were already inside the main hall. More were pouring in. It was only the next day that we were able to piece together the story:

A little before 10 o'clock, a man, heavily bandaged, had been brought to Gandhiji's residence by some excited young men at the head of a procession.

Gandhiji had gone to bed.

As he recalled later:

> They began to shout at the top of their voices. My sleep was disturbed but I tried to lie quiet, not knowing what was happening. I heard the window panes being smashed. I had on either side of me two very brave girls (Abha and Manu). They would not (wake me up from my) sleep, but without my knowledge—for my eyes were closed —they went among the crowd and tried to pacify them. Thank God, the crowd did not harm them.

The entreaties of the two girls apparently had no effect on the rowdies. They began to smash furniture, picture frames and chandeliers with hockey sticks and by hurling stones. There were two groups—one trying to incite, the other to pacify the rowdies. The sensible section tried their best to protect the two girls and entreated them to go inside.

To resume Gandhiji's narrative:

> The old Muslim lady in the house endearingly called Bi Amma (mother) and a young Muslim stood near my matting, I suppose, to protect me from suspecting harm. The noise continued to swell. Some had entered the central hall, and begun to knock open the many doors. I felt that I must get up and face the angry crowd. I stood at

the threshold of one of the doors. Friendly faces surrounded me and would not let me move forward.

Gandhiji's vow of silence admitted of his breaking it on such occasions. He addressed the rowdies: "What madness is this? Why do you not attack me? I offer myself for attack." He repeated it thrice and asked his Bengali granddaughter-in-law to translate his words into Bengali.

All to no purpose. They wouldn't listen to any reasoning. I clasped my hands in the Hindu fashion. Nothing doing. More window panes began to crack.

"Where is the rascal Suhrawardy?" shouted someone from among the crowd. It seems they intended to lynch Suhrawardy. Luckily he was not in the house. He had gone home to get ready to start with me for Noakhali. Not finding him, they turned their wrath on me. There was pandemonium.

Just then two Muslim members of the household, with whom Gandhiji was staying, came rushing in, pursued by the infuriated crowd. One of them was bleeding profusely. He took shelter behind Gandhiji. Seeing him, someone aimed a massive brickbat at him. It struck a Muslim standing by. A heavy stick narrowly missed Gandhiji's head and crashed against the opposite wall without hurting anybody. Had it hit Gandhji, it would have been the end.

At last, Gandhiji said in a husky voice: "My God asks me, 'Where do you stand?' I am deeply pained. Is this the reality of the peace that was established on 15th August?"

Minutes later, the police chief and his officers came in. They appealed to Gandhiji to retire. In an aside I requested them not to use force against the rowdies, knowing how it would affect Gandhiji. After putting in some efforts they succeeded in getting the building cleared of the crowd.

Gandhiji called Charu and me and said: "My resolve to go to Noakhali collapses after this. You will agree I cannot leave for Noakhali or for that matter for anywhere else under these circumstances."

It was 12:30 when Gandhiji went to bed. But the crowd outside lingered on in the streets till long after that. Ultimately, the police had to use tear gas to disperse it. By the time silence was fully restored, it was 1:30 in the morning. Not till 2 o'clock could anyone go to sleep.

* * *

The news of the previous night's happenings had gone round the whole city with incredible speed. Charu Chowdhury and I, fearing a very serious reaction in Noakhali if the situation deteriorated any further in Calcutta, decided to approach the Hindu Mahasabha leaders and plead with them for their cooperation in Gandhiji and Suhrawardy's peace effort.

We first called on Dr Shyama Prasad Mookerjee. He was suffering from acute gallbladder trouble and had been recommended complete bed rest. We told him that if the minority community in Noakhali, or for that matter in the whole of East Bengal, was not to be exposed to an incalculable risk, the situation in Calcutta had to be immediately brought under control. He listened to us with utmost attention. At the end, he said: "I shall certainly issue an appeal and do anything else you might suggest." He asked us to come an hour later, when he would be ready with his statement. His action followed accordingly.

When we returned to the Hydari Mansion, we found Gandhiji writing a letter to Dr Mookerjee to ask whether it was not time that he issued an appeal to the Hindus of Calcutta. His face lit up as I handed him Dr Mookerjee's draft statement. With some minor changes it was released to the Press the next day:

> The continuance of peaceful conditions in West Bengal and East Bengal is essential for peace in India. Calcutta is the key to the situation. If it is at peace, it must influence East Bengal. Peace in the whole of Bengal must again affect the whole of the Punjab. The majority community in Bengal must realize, the senseless oppression of innocent members of the minority community does not pay and creates a vicious circle which one cannot cut through.

At about two in the afternoon, news came that a violent communal conflagration had broken out simultaneously in several parts of the city. Every 10 minutes, fresh reports of incidents kept pouring in and with every fresh report Gandhiji's self-introspection grew deeper.

He used to have fruit juice every afternoon. That day when it was brought to him, he waved it away.

The day's news had created panic among the poorer Muslim inhabitants of Beliaghata who, on the strength of Gandhiji's previous assurances, had already returned to their homes. A batch of them boarded an open truck to flee to the nearest Muslim locality. As the truck carrying them passed by Gandhiji's residence, hand-grenades were hurled upon it from the roof of an adjoining building and two Muslims were instantaneously killed.

As soon as Gandhiji heard of the incident, he expressed a desire to go and see the victims. It was a piteous sight. The dead men lay in a pool of blood, their eyes glazed and a swarm of flies was buzzing over their wounds. They must have been poor day-labourers. One of them was clad in a tattered *dhoti* (traditional garment of men's wear in India). A four-*anna* piece had rolled out of his cloth and lay near his dead body. Gandhiji stood like one transfixed at the sight of this cold-blooded butchery of innocent men.

Gandhiji to Sardar Patel   1st September, 1947
I hear that conflagration has burst out at many places. What was regarded as the "Calcutta miracle" has proved to be a nine-days' wonder. I am pondering what my duty is in the circumstances.

The evening prayer, held indoors, was still in progress when Suhrawardy with NC Chatterji and several leading Marwari businessmen came in. They all admitted that the Hindus had completely lost control of their actions.

A Marwari friend asked, "How can we help?"

Gandhiji advised, "You should go in the midst of the flames and prevent them from spreading or get killed in the attempt. A number of you are businessmen of repute in the city. At least in the localities where you carry on your business your presence should tell. But in any case, do not return alive to report failure."

Even while he was speaking to these friends, he was asking himself the question, "Have I the right to give vicarious advice to others so long as I have not set the example myself?" Speaking aloud, he said:

"The situation calls for sacrifice on the part of top rankers. Hitherto, with a couple of exceptions, the nameless rank-and-file have been the victims of the holocaust. That is not enough."

After the visitors had left, he went out for his usual evening walk. Before he returned to the house, he knew what he had to do. The terrific mental strain had given him acute diarrhoea. After taking a glass of hot water and glucose, he sat down to draft the statement embodying his decision.

When Rajaji came in at 10 pm, Gandhiji showed him his draft. Glancing through it Rajaji, with his usual affectionate banter, remarked: "Can one fast against the goondas?"

Gandhiji replied: "I want to touch the hearts of those who are behind the goondas. The hearts of the goondas may or may not be touched. It would be enough for my purpose if they realize that society at large has no sympathy with their aims or methods and that the peace-loving element is determined to assert itself or perish in the attempt."

In the draft, Gandhiji had reserved to himself the liberty to add sour lime juice to water during the fast to make the water drinkable. He had developed a queer allergy to plain water ever since his first 14 days' fast in South Africa. It brought on nausea.

Rajaji asked him: "Why add sour lime juice to water if you are to put yourself entirely in God's hands?"

"You are right," Gandhiji said. "I allowed it out of weakness. It jarred on me even as I wrote it. A *satyagrahi* must hope to survive his fast only by the timely fulfillment of the terms of his fast."

And so the portion referring to the sour lime juice was scored out and the unadulterated venture of faith commenced. It was past 11 when Rajaji left with the final statement. It was released to the Press the same night. After referring to the disturbances at the Hydari Mansion on the night of 31st August, it went on:

> There is no way of keeping the peace in Calcutta or elsewhere if the elementary rule of civilized society is not observed. The recognition of the golden rule of never taking the law into one's own hands has no exceptions.
>
> Now that the Calcutta bubble seems to have burst, with what face can I go to the Punjab? The weapon which has hitherto proved

infallible for me is fasting. To put an appearance before a yelling crowd does not always work. It certainly did not last night. What my word in person cannot do, my fast may. It may touch the hearts of all the warring elements in the Punjab if it does in Calcutta. I, therefore, begin fasting from 8.15 tonight to end only as and when sanity returns to Calcutta. I shall, as usual, permit myself to add salt and soda bicarbonate to the water I may wish to drink during the fast.

If the people of Calcutta wish me to proceed to the Punjab and help the people there, they have to enable me to break the fast as early as may be.

* * *

On the second day of the fast, someone brought a report that looting had continued till midnight. But since then, it had been all quiet.

Gandhiji's reply was: "No wonder, the looters also needed rest after the full day's work!"

Communal frenzy exacted its toll of sacrifice from two workers who dared to live up to the creed of non-violence. Sachin Mittra, aged 38, an MA of Calcutta University and a seasoned *satyagrahi*, was a trusted worker under Thakkar Bapa in the Noakhali peace mission. Gifted with a keen aesthetic sense and amiable nature, he had endeared himself to all his companions. On the 1st September, on hearing of the conflagration in the city, at the invitation of a few Muslim friends, he set out with them in the direction of Nakhoda mosque, which was reported to be a danger spot. At a crossroad, the party was surrounded by a hostile Muslim crowd. The rowdies separated Sachin and his Hindu colleagues from their Muslim comrades. Sachin was stabbed and the others severely assaulted. Their Muslim comrades tried to protect them but were overpowered and some of them sustained injuries. Sachin was removed to the hospital where he succumbed to his wounds—a victim of fanatical fury which, in its deluded ignorance, strikes down the very hand that was held up to protect it.

The other worker who paid with his life was Smritish Bannerjee. Of the same age as Sachin Mittra, on learning that a peace procession of schoolboys and girls was in danger, he rushed to the area. But later, when the procession was attacked, he was seen with a blood-stained shirt trying to escort some girls to a place of safety. Later, his body was brought to the hospital with five mortal stab wounds.

Gandhiji refused to mourn the two deaths. In a note to Angshu Rani Mittra, Sachin's widow, he wrote: "Pyarelalji has just given me the news that your husband who was mortally stabbed in the course of protecting others has succumbed to his wounds today. Do not let this be an occasion for sorrow but only for joy. Sachin has become immortal. You must not grieve but lose yourself in service in emulation of him."

At midday, a group of ladies came. They wanted the dead body of Sachin Mittra to be taken out in a procession. Gandhiji deprecated the idea, saying he hated too much being made of the physical body. "If anybody tried to take out my body in a procession after I died, I would certainly tell them—if my corpse could speak—to spare me and cremate me where I had died."

* * *

The third day of the fast dawned with Gandhiji growing weaker. The voice had sunk to a mere whisper, the pulse was small and rapid. There was a feeling of giddiness on getting up and a buzzing sound in the ears.

Then the miracle happened. As the leaden hours crept by and slowly life ebbed out of the frail little man on the fasting bed, it caused a deep heart-churning in all concerned, bringing the hidden lie to the surface. People came and confessed to him what they would have confided to no mortal ear. Hindus and Muslims combined in an all-out effort to save the precious life that was being offered as ransom for disrupted peace between brother and brother. Mixed processions, consisting of all communities, paraded through the affected parts of the city to restore communal harmony.

At midday, a party of 27 people from central Calcutta came and met Gandhiji. They were members of what had come to be known as "resistance groups" that had sprung up as an answer to hooliganism during and after the Muslim League "Direct Action" in 1946. They were said to be in control of the turbulent elements in the city. Admitting that they had taken part in the killing, they begged for forgiveness and requested him to give up the fast. Their faces wore a penitent look, not unmixed with shame. They gave an undertaking that they would immediately bring the troublemakers under control. They said they had already traced and put under restraint the ringleaders, who had organized the rowdy demonstration in the Hydari Mansion on Sunday last, including the person who had hurled the stick that had narrowly missed hitting him. (Later the assailant came to Gandhiji and asked to be forgiven.) They would all surrender themselves to him and take whatever punishment he might mete out to them. Would not Gandhiji on the strength of that assurance now break his fast? "We shall then be able to go to work unburdened by the oppression of the fast." If not, what was Gandhiji's condition for breaking the fast?

But Gandhiji felt himself unable to accede to their request. He told them he would break his fast only when his instinct told him that stable peace had been established in the city. They would have to assure him that there never would be a recrudescence of communal madness in the city even though the whole of West Bengal, and for that matter India, went up in flames. The Muslims should be able to tell him that they now felt safe and, therefore, he need not prolong his fast.

At 6 pm when Gandhiji, who had dozed off for a while, woke up, a deputation of the citizens of Calcutta representing all communities waited on him. Included in it were Shaheed Suhrawardy, NC Chatterji and Sardar Niranjan Singh Talib. They told him that they had been to all affected parts of the city and there was quiet everywhere. They would hold themselves responsible for anything untoward that might happen thereafter. They had every reason to hope that there would be no recrudescence of trouble which they maintained was "really not communal" but "the work of the goondas". They requested him to terminate his fast.

After some reflection Gandhiji spoke. He deprecated the suggestion that the outbreak of violence was not communal in character but really the work of the goondas. "It is we who make the goondas and we alone can unmake them. Goondas never act on their own. By themselves they cannot function." It was the cowardice or passive sympathy of the average citizen or "the man with a stake", that gave the so-called goondas the power to do mischief. "My fast should make you more vigilant, more truthful, more careful, and more precise in the language you use. You have all come here out of affection for me to ask me to give up my fast. But before I can accede to your request, I want to ask you two questions: Can you, in all sincerity, assure me that there never will be a repetition of trouble in Calcutta? Can you say that there is a genuine change of heart among the citizens so that they will no longer tolerate, much less foster communal frenzy? And if trouble breaks out—since you are not omnipotent or even omniscient—would you give me your word of honour that you would not live to report failure but lay down your life in the attempt to protect those whose safety you are pledging?"

Rajaji and Acharya Kripalani, who had arrived during the latter part of the discussion, proposed that they might leave Gandhiji alone for a little to confer among themselves. The leaders then retired to the next room for consultation and remained there for nearly half an hour.

The strain of speaking had utterly exhausted Gandhiji. Suddenly he felt giddy. Tossing about restlessly in his bed, he began to recite *Ramanama.*

In the adjoining room, Rajaji dictated the draft of the pledge which was signed first by NC Chatterji and DN Mukherjee of the Hindu Mahasabha, followed by Shaheed Suhrawardy as the leader of the Muslim League Parliamentary Party of West Bengal, RK Jaidka, the Punjabi leader and Niranjan Singh Talib, the Sikh leader. Without any further loss of time the signatories returned to Gandhiji.

The document ran: "We the undersigned promise to Gandhiji that now that peace and quiet have been restored in Calcutta once again, we shall never allow communal strife in the city and shall strive unto death to prevent it."

Before breaking the fast, Gandhiji addressed a few words to the gathering: "I am breaking this fast so that I might be able to do something for the Punjab. I have accepted your assurance at its face value. I hope and pray I shall never have to regret it. I would certainly like to live to serve India and humanity, but I do not wish to be duped into prolonging my life."

Seventy-three hours after it was commenced, Gandhiji broke the fast, at 9.15 pm on the 4th September, by slowly sipping a glass of diluted orange juice. It was preceded by a short prayer, in which all present joined, followed by the singing of Tagore's song:

> When the heart is hard and parched up,
> Come upon me with a shower of mercy.

The orange juice was handed to him by Shaheed Suhrawardy, who bowed at his feet and wept.

A truckload of hand-grenades and arms had in the meantime arrived to be surrendered to Gandhiji as a token of repentance on the part of those who had taken part in the savagery of reprisals and counter-reprisals.

Before the leaders had dispersed, Gandhiji called Rajaji to his side and said, "I am thinking of leaving for the Punjab tomorrow."

Rajaji was in a fix. If the idea took hold of Gandhiji, it would be difficult to dislodge him from it. Suhrawardy tactfully came to the rescue: "Sir, you cannot leave Calcutta without giving the citizens of Calcutta an opportunity to join you in a public prayer and thanksgiving. If we tried tomorrow, it would be simply impossible to control the delirious crowd. At the earliest it can be on the day after tomorrow." Others supported him. They did not tell him what was uppermost in their minds, namely, that they were deeply concerned about his undertaking a thousand-mile railway journey within 24 hours of his breaking the fast, with enthusiastic crowds all along the line.

The next day still another dump of country-made arms—guns, swords, daggers and cartridges—was similarly surrendered.

Suhrawardy came at midday. Their joint mission had ended. What were Gandhiji's orders for him next—he asked.

Gandhiji said: "If your conversion is sincere, do not again let yourself be tempted by power."

At the evening prayer gathering on the 6th September, Gandhiji repeated the warning he had given to the leaders at the time of the breaking of his fast. Suhrawardy, after seconding Gandhiji's appeal, announced that he would be joining Gandhiji in his Punjab mission.

He had put himself unreservedly under Mahatmaji's order. Thereafter, he would carry out his biddings.

On Gandhiji's last day in Calcutta some ladies came to bid him farewell by performing *arti*—the centuries-old ceremonial Hindu way of expressing devotion. The ceremony consists of waving lights fed with pure ghee round the head of the object of adoration. As they approached him bearing the salver on which the lights were placed, he stopped them. "Put out the lights, drain every drop of ghee into a vessel and distribute it to the poor," he said.

At 9 pm, he boarded the train for Delhi. Among those who saw him off were the Chief Minister of West Bengal with his fellow-ministers and Shaheed Suhrawardy. Reverentially, they took leave one after another. As the train started, Suhrawardy's eyes were wet with tears —perhaps for the first time in his life appearing in public like that.

* * *

In November 1946, Gandhiji had served the Bihar Muslims from East Bengal. He now served the Hindus of Noakhali by staying to serve the Muslims of Calcutta though the call from Noakhali rang in his ears. From Calcutta, he set out for the bleeding Punjab. But he could not get there either. Delhi claimed him. Through his stay in Delhi he was able to serve the whole of India and Pakistan.

Never did he show himself to greater advantage than during those fateful days when, like a Titan, he rushed from one danger spot to another to prop up the crumbling heavens. His daily utterances at his prayer meetings, his simple "yes" and "no" gestures, even his silences became commands, watchwords, orders for the day, to bring the frail ship of India's independence safely to port through the storm-tossed waters that lay ahead.

11

CITY OF THE DEAD

On the morning of the 9th September, 1947, Gandhiji arrived in Delhi, never to leave again. Communal riots had broken out in the capital. Delhi had become the city of the dead.

He was motored to Birla House. The sweepers' colony, where he used to stay, was occupied by the refugees from the West Punjab. A 24-hour curfew was in force in the city. The military had been called, but firing and looting had not stopped altogether. The streets were littered with the dead.

On either side of the border in the two Punjabs, life was becoming impossible for the minorities. Anti-social elements were abroad, defying all authority and destroying the very structure of society. The atmosphere in Delhi had grown more and more tense as refugees poured in from West Punjab. They brought with them gruesome tales—whole villages devastated, women dishonoured, carried away, distributed as "booty", sometimes openly sold. Infants in arms and children had been speared to death in cold blood. There were wholesale forcible conversions. Arson and loot were rampant. Refugee convoys and trains were attacked. Often these stories were exaggerated. What had happened in Delhi was for the most part a reaction to these accounts.

The Delhi Province was declared a dangerously disturbed area. Orders were issued to the police and armed forces to shoot to kill the law-breakers. The infliction the death penalty was permitted for offences like attempt to murder, abduction, arson and looting. The civil authority in both the Punjabs was paralyzed. The communal virus had infiltrated the army and the police. Muslim troops would not fire on their co-religionists, nor would the Hindus and Sikhs fire on theirs.

In the tornado of primitive passions that had broken loose, millions had been uprooted and thrown into turmoil, like forest leaves caught in a hurricane. The biggest migration of population in history was in progress. Almost ten million people were on the move in both directions across the border in the Punjab.

All modes of transport were employed for the evacuation of refugees—trains, cars and airplanes. But these could only make a small dent into the problem. The only effective way of moving such large numbers was by route marches. These marches were in progress in both directions. To avoid clashes, block timings had been mutually arranged between the authorities on both sides.

Feeding, clothing and housing these millions; the control of epidemics that might break out for lack of proper sanitary arrangements and medical relief; and the prevention of inevitable clashes between the incoming refugees—their minds almost unhinged by the privations they had suffered—and the minorities still on both sides, these and many others were problems of baffling magnitude and complexity.

People wondered if he would repeat in Delhi the miracle he had wrought in Calcutta. All eyes were on Gandhiji. But his own were turned inward. At last he said: "I do not know what I shall be able to do here. But one thing is clear. *I cannot leave this place until Delhi is peaceful again.*"

Some Muslims came to see him and wept as they narrated to him their tales of woe. He consoled them. They must be brave. He was there in Delhi to "Do or Die".

In a statement to the Press, he said:

I am prepared to understand the anger of the refugees, whom fate had driven from West Punjab. But anger is just short of madness. Retaliation is no remedy. It makes the original disease worse.

* * *

At noon, news came that refugees were about to attack the Tuberculosis Hospital opposite Kingsway refugee camp, where there was a large number of Muslim patients. Gandhiji asked Sushila to proceed there. He briefed her: "On your way, stop at the Secretariat and inform Sardar and Jawaharlal where I am sending you."

Sardar was not in his office but she saw Nehru. He asked her to accompany him in his car. At the Town Hall he asked the Deputy Commissioner to rush a guard to the hospital. The Deputy Commissioner said he could do nothing. All the guards were out on duty. Nehru said, "All right, then I shall send Sushila to guard them." And with a fatherly pat on the back he pushed her into the car.

On her way, she saw a mosque in flames. She stopped to see if there was anyone inside. As she stood there, a shower of bullets came from the building opposite. It was a stronghold of the Rashtriya Swayam-sevak Sangh. The bullets were evidently intended to kill the Muslims prowling about the mosque.

On reaching the hospital, she found that the patients had just been evacuated, with Lady Mountbatten's help, to Juma Mosque. On the road, she saw some refugees getting away with looted goods in the direction of the Kingsway camp. "What are you doing here?" she shouted at a policeman who was ambling a few yards behind. "Don't you see it is looted property? Can't you stop them?" Giving a casual, apathetic look, the policeman replied: "Bigger men than I cannot stop this. What can I do?"

Just then another car pulled up from behind. Nehru, having sent Sushila to the hospital, had been worrying about her. After attending to some urgent business, he followed her. She recounted the conversation with the policeman. Nehru was very angry and drove towards the camp. He jumped out of the car as it approached the refugees with their loot. A crowd gathered around as they recognized him. He scolded them: "I thought we were helping our suffering brethren. I did not know we were sheltering thieves and dacoits."

The crowd scowled. They also were angry. A fiery young man came forward and said: "You lecture to us! Do you know what we have suffered?" Nehru could contain himself no longer. He shook the young man by the scruff of his neck. Sushila felt anxious. Supposing the crowd got out of hand? She tried to pull him away. As he released his hold on the young man, the latter muttered, "Yes, Panditji, go on. What better luck can I expect than to die at your hands?"

Nehru's wrath melted away. His face was sad; his voice full of emotion. "This is not the time for me to tell you how much," he said, "my heart aches at your suffering. But what I say to you is this: Have these Muslims done you any harm? If not, then you must not injure them. We must be just. If justice requires it and it is necessary, we can go to war with Pakistan and you can enlist. But this kind of thing is degrading and cowardly."

The crowd cheered wildly: "*Jawaharlal Nehru zindabad* (Long live Jawaharlal Nehru)."

* * *

Gandhiji set out to make a tour of the riot-affected parts of the city and the various Muslim and Hindu refugee camps.

He also went to the Jamia Millia Islamia—the Muslim National University. Muslim men and women from the surrounding villages had taken shelter there. For two days they had lived in hourly danger of death. But there was courage and faith in the words of Dr Zakir Husain, the Vice-Chancellor of the Jamia. A few days earlier, while returning from the Punjab, he had been surrounded by a hostile crowd at Jullunder railway station and was saved only by the providential arrival of a Sikh captain and another Hindu friend who recognized him and protected him at considerable risk to themselves. He was sad but not bitter.

But Gandhiji felt sick at heart. If even a person like Dr Zakir Husain was not safe, what was life worth in India?

Angry faces surrounded him at a Hindu refugee camp, which he visited on his way back. Some Hindu and Sikh refugees accused him of having more sympathy for the Muslims than for them. There was a strange, sad look on Gandhiji's face. They had a right to be angry, he said. They were the real sufferers.

There were thousands upon thousands of them in various camps, herded together like cattle, lacking even elementary decencies of life, not to speak of food, clothing or shelter. Misery was writ large on their faces. Gandhiji suffered with them. But they could not see it. Their wounds were fresh and bleeding; revenge seemed sweet to many. One of them was heard to say that so far they had only avenged half an *anna* in the rupee, but now that "the old man" had come, they would not be able to square up their account. Yet they clung to him. There was something in him which drew them to him in spite of themselves. They might be angry with him, even quarrel with him, but in their heart of hearts they knew that he was the friend of all and enemy of none; he loved them and theirs with a love greater than they themselves were, perhaps, capable of. They wanted him to guide them even when they were not prepared to follow his advice.

In the course of his evening post-prayer address, Gandhiji declared that it would not do for either dominion to plead helplessness and say that it was all the work of the ruffians. Each dominion had to bear full responsibility for the acts of those who lived in it.

Were the Indian Ministers to declare their bankruptcy and shamelessly own to the world that the people of Delhi or the refugees would not voluntarily obey the rule of the land? He would like their Ministers to break, rather than bend in the attempt to wean the people from their madness.

The head of the Rashtriya Swayam-sevak Sangh also called upon Gandhiji. It was common knowledge that the RSS had been behind the bulk of the killings in various parts of India. This, these friends denied. Their organization was for protecting Hinduism—not for killing Muslims. It was not hostile to anyone. It stood for peace.

This was laying it a bit thick. But Gandhiji, with his boundless faith in human nature and in the redemptive power of truth, felt he must give everybody a chance to make good his bona fides. It was something that at least they did not glory in wrongdoing. They should issue a public statement, he told them, repudiating the allegations against them and openly condemning the killing and harassment of the Muslims that had taken place and that was still going on in the city. They said Gandhiji could do that himself on their behalf, on the strength of what they had told him. Gandhiji answered that he would certainly do that but if what they were saying was sincerely meant, it was better that the public should have it from their own lips.

A member of Gandhiji's party interjected that the RSS people had done a fine job at the Wah refugee camp. They had shown discipline, courage and capacity for hard work. "But don't forget," answered Gandhiji, "even so had Hitler's Nazis and the Fascists under Mussolini." He characterized the RSS as a "communal body with a totalitarian outlook."

A few days later, the RSS leaders took Gandhiji to attend one of their rallies. In welcoming Gandhiji, the RSS leader described him as "a great man that Hinduism has produced." In his reply, Gandhiji made it obvious that while he was certainly proud of being a Hindu, his Hinduism was neither intolerant nor exclusive. The beauty of Hinduism as he understood it was that it absorbed the best there was in all faiths. If Hindus believed that in India there was no place for non-Hindus on equal and honourable terms and Muslims, if they wanted to live in India, had to be content with an inferior status; or if the Muslims thought that in Pakistan Hindus could live only as a subject race, it would mean an eclipse of Hinduism and an eclipse of Islam. He was glad, therefore, he said, to have their assurance that their policy was not of antagonism towards Islam. He warned them that, if the charge that their organization was behind the killing of the Muslims was correct, it would come to a bad end.

Gandhiji was asked whether Hinduism did not permit the killing of evildoers.

One had to be an infallible judge, said Gandhiji, as to who was the evildoer before the question of killing could arise. In other words, one had to be completely faultless before such a right could accrue to one. How could a sinner claim the right to judge or execute another sinner?

There was a big crowd at the prayer meeting at Kingsway camp. As soon as the recitation from the Koran commenced, someone in the gathering shouted: "To the recitation of these verses our mothers and sisters were dishonoured, our dear ones killed. We will not let you recite these verses here."

Some shouted *"Gandhi murdabad* (Death to Gandhi)." All efforts to restore order failed. As a result, the prayer had to be abandoned. As he withdrew, stones were thrown at his car.

* * *

Gandhiji visited the Muslim refugee camp at Purana Quila. There were about 75,000 Muslim refugees awaiting there to be evacuated to Pakistan.

The refugees were in a very ugly mood. As soon as Gandhiji's car entered the gate, crowds rushed out of their tents and surrounded it. Anti-Gandhi slogans were shouted. Someone from among the crowd violently opened the door of Gandhiji's car. One of the friends who had taken Gandhiji to the camp asked the driver to take the car out of the camp by the nearest gate. The driver pressed the pedal and the car shot forward. But Gandhiji ordered him to stop. He wanted to face the angry crowd, he said. Immediately, the refugees came running up and again surrounded the car. While his companion helplessly looked on, Gandhiji stepped out. The crowd closed in upon him. He asked them to assemble on the lawn. Some sat down. Those on the fringes kept standing and, full of anger, gesticulated menacingly. Some Muslim volunteers tried to pacify them.

Anxious moments followed. There was no loudspeaker arrangement and Gandhiji's feeble voice could not carry far. Leaning upon the shoulders of one of his companions, he asked him to repeat his words at the top of his voice. At first, the refugees were inclined to be rude. When he said that there was one God for all—"to me there are no distinctions of Hindu, Muslim, Christian and Sikh, they are all one to me"—there were shouts of angry protest. He entreated them to be calm and shed anger and fear. God would set right what man had spoilt. For his part he had come here to "Do or Die", he concluded.

There was nothing new in the words, but they heard the passion in his voice and saw in the agonizing, resigned look on that worn out face how deeply he felt for and suffered with them and all those who suffered. Scowling ceased. Soon tears were trickling down the cheeks of some. They narrated to him the tale of their hardships and sufferings. He listened to them with deep sympathy and promised to do all he could for them. Those who were thirsting for his blood a few moments earlier, were now his friends. They respectfully escorted him to his car and stood there in silence as it passed out of the camp with him, his hands folded to bid them goodbye and furrows of deep pain on his face.

A group of Congress workers came to Gandhiji a few days later and said, "Give us orders." He had orders for them. Delhi's sanitary arrangements were nearing a collapse, decomposing corpses still filled the streets and bylanes with stink. Some sweepers had been brought from Meerut to work in Purana Quila. But they were so frightened by the conditions there that they begged to be sent back to their homes. Gandhiji asked the Congress workers to organize themselves into scavenging squads. "If in the course of your work, some of you should get killed, it will be your crowning glory and I shall congratulate you and the Congress organization on it."

* * *

On the night of 14th September, Delhi experienced one of its worst thunderstorms. The rain fell in bucketfuls and the sky was rent by incessant sheet-lightning. As Gandhiji lay awake in bed listening to what should have been the soothing sound of life-giving rain, his thoughts went out to those thousands of refugees—men, women and children—who, foodless and under the bare skies, must at places have been in knee-deep water in the various refugee camps, and to others outside on their long, weary treks. Was all that inevitable? In a written message to his evening prayer gathering the next day, he said:

Have the citizens of Delhi gone mad? Have they no humanity left in them? Has love of the country and its freedom no appeal for them?

The people of Delhi will make it difficult to demand justice from the Pakistan Government if they take the law into their own hands. Those who seek justice must do justice, must have clean hands.

It was true, the Hindus and the Sikhs were treated badly in Pakistan, he continued. But it was no less true that in the East Punjab also the Muslims had been treated likewise. All were guilty to the same magnitude. Guilt could not be measured in golden scales.

* * *

In the second half of September, huge foot convoys of non-Muslims, each 30,000 to 40,000 strong, started from the fertile canal colonies of West Punjab upon a 150-miles trek. From the 18th September to the 20th October, 24 of these, altogether 8,49,000 strong, flanked by their cattle and bullock-carts crossed over to India. An astonishing phenomenon was the movement of some 2,00,000 refugees, mostly Sikhs, from Lyallpur, in a column 57 miles long. On the way, fleeing refugees, whether they travelled by road, by rail, or on foot, were attacked by the people from the surrounding villages. Outbreak of cholera and other epidemics and later floods added to their misery. Many thousands thus perished on the way.

Settling the incoming refugees in the deserted Muslim houses or other Muslim buildings suggested itself as an easy and ready-made solution. The communalist section openly advocated this course and incited the non-Muslim refugees to occupy the Muslim vacant houses and terrorize and turn out the rest from their homes.

One evening, Gandhiji paid a visit to Daryaganj—a predominantly Muslim quarter. The Muslims of the locality wept as they complained to him of the partisan behaviour of the military and the police which might, after all, compel them to leave their homes and go out of Delhi. Gandhiji told them that they must, under no circumstances, leave their homes. "Even if the police and the military should open fire upon you, you should face the bullets and bravely die but not flee from your homes." If they lived as law-abiding, honest and loyal citizens, no one could force them out.

The Muslims gave Gandhiji a written declaration that they would be loyal to the Indian Union. If necessary, they would even fight under the banner of the Union. "How can I discount your profession of loyalty made to me on solemn oath?" Gandhiji said to them. "I must trust you. On your part, you should trust the Union Government."

Concluding, he further advised them that, as a token of their loyalty to the Indian Union, they should issue a public statement that all Hindu women abducted by the Muslims in Pakistan should be restored to their families. They should unequivocally condemn the Pakistan Government where it had departed from civilized conduct and demand that all those Hindus and Sikhs who had had to leave their homes in Pakistan should be invited to return with full guarantee of their safety and self-respect.

A number of Sikh refugees from West Punjab came to Gandhiji. Some of them wept as they narrated to him how their womenfolk had been dishonoured.

Gandhiji asked one of them: "You saw it happen with your own eyes?"

The refugee answered: "Yes, with our own eyes."

Gandhiji's reply followed: "And you have lived to report this? I feel now more strongly than ever that the only guarantee of protection of a woman's honour is for her to learn to prefer death to dishonour."

In the evening he visited Kucha Tarachand, a Hindu pocket surrounded on all sides by Muslims. The Hindus gave a highly exaggerated recital of their suffering and ended by saying that the whole locality should be cleared of Muslims as West Pakistan had been of the Hindus.

Gandhiji replied that he could never associate himself with such a demand. Two wrongs could not make one right. His advice to them was that they should fill their hearts with courage and be proud to live fearlessly in the midst of a large Muslim population, just as he had been asking the Muslims to live in the midst of the Hindu majority.

At a prayer meeting, Gandhiji remarked that he was unable to accept the contention that the administration could not prevent the non-Muslims from forcibly occupying Muslim houses, evacuated or otherwise, as a democratic Government could not use force against overwhelming public sentiment. If the people would not let the Government do the right thing, the Government should resign. Similarly, those who wanted all Muslims to be driven out of India could ask for the resignation of their Government, but they must not obstruct the Government efforts or resort to lawlessness; that would be a negation of democracy.

Surely it was cowardly on the part of the majority to kill or banish the minority for fear that the latter would all turn traitor. "Robust faith in oneself and brave trust in the opponent is the best safeguard. Therefore, I plead with all earnestness that Delhi should forget what Pakistan is doing. Then only can it claim the proud privilege of having broken the vicious circle of private revenge and retaliation."

* * *

The ceaseless physical and spiritual strain in Delhi had begun to exact its toll from Gandhiji. For some time he had been suffering from a severe attack of whooping cough and flu. His temperature rose to 102° one day. But he would neither stop giving interviews nor discontinue his spinning. "What use is my life if I cannot even console the afflicted by listening to their tale of distress, since I can do nothing more for them?" It was proposed that the number of interviews might be restricted for the time being. But he would not hear of that either. He preferred to die in harness, he said, serving the people with his last breath.

The cough was at its worst at night. The seizures were sometimes so frequent and prolonged that words barely came through and those in attendance found it difficult to follow what he was saying. Owing to the strain of persistent coughing, there was tenderness in the abdomen and streaks of blood appeared in the sputum.

The nurse on duty one morning did not have the heart to wake him up at prayer time as he was having a quiet, restful sleep after many nights of wakefulness. He was deeply distressed. False pity was a dereliction of duty, he told her. It would have been real affection to wake him up at the appointed time.

Giving his reason for his refusal to take regular medical treatment, to which the prolongation of his cough was attributed by the doctors, he said that he did not doubt the efficacy of medical treatment for the cure of certain physical ailments. But he felt that, in the midst of the flames that surrounded him on all sides, there was all the greater need for a burning faith in God. Hence his reliance on the power of the *Ramanama* alone.

* * *

The 2nd of October, 1947, was Gandhiji's birthday—the last to be celebrated during his lifetime. He observed it, as usual, by fasting, praying and extra spinning.

Visitors and friends continued to come all day to offer homage to the Father of the Nation. His request to all was to pray that "either the present conflagration should end or He should take me away. I do not wish another birthday to overtake me in an India still in flames."

The occasion burnt itself on to the memories of the visitors as one of the saddest in Gandhiji's life. "What sin must I have committed," he remarked to Sardar, "that He should have kept me alive to witness all these horrors?"

He seemed to be consumed by the feeling of helplessness in the face of the surrounding conflagration. "The desire to live for 125 years has completely vanished as a result of this continued fratricide. I do not want to be a helpless witness to it."

There was nothing but agony in his heart. His was a lone voice. He could not live while hatred and killing choked the atmosphere. He pleaded with the people to give up the madness that had seized them and purge their hearts of hatred.

* * *

The 11th of October was Gandhiji's birthday according to the Hindu calendar. The Gujaratis of Delhi had arranged a reception to present him with a purse which they had collected to commemorate his birthday. Gandhiji was still suffering from his cold and flu, but agreed to attend the meeting. When Sardar came to take him to the meeting, he was having a spasm of whooping cough. Sardar chaffed him: "There is no end to your greed! To collect a purse you will leave even your deathbed!"

"Sardar will not miss a laugh even at the foot of the gallows," exclaimed Gandhiji.

12

ANVIL OF CONSCIENCE

Gandhiji's voice was heard for the last time in the All-India Congress Committee. In a straight-from-the-shoulder talk, every exhortation was a sledge-hammer blow aimed at the anvil of their conscience to strike the fire of the old Congress tradition and the ideals that had made the Congress a power without a rival in the land:

There are many places where a Muslim cannot live in security. We have to fight against this insanity and find a cure for it. I confess that I have not yet found it.

Some say that if we perpetrate worse atrocities on Muslims here than those perpetrated on Hindus and Sikhs in Pakistan, it will teach the Muslims in Pakistan a salutary lesson. They will, indeed, be taught a lesson, but what will happen to you in the meanwhile? The wicked sink under the weight of their own evil. Must we sink with them?

I hold it to be an impossibility that three and a half crores of Muslims can be driven away to Pakistan. What crime have they committed? The Muslim League may have been culpable, but not every Muslim. If you think that they are all traitors and fifth-columnists, shoot them by all means; but to assume that they are all criminals because they are Muslims, is wrong. If you bully them, beat them, and threaten them, what can they do but run away to Pakistan? But such conduct is unworthy of you. Thereby, you will degrade the Congress, degrade your religion and degrade the nation.

144

If you realize this, then it is your duty to call back all those Muslims who have been obliged to flee to Pakistan. India is big enough to keep them as well as all the Hindu and Sikh refugees who have fled here from Pakistan. Of course, those Muslims who believe in Pakistan and wish to seek their happiness there are welcome to migrate.

As things are, we cannot hold our heads high in the world today and we have to confess that we have been obliged to copy Pakistan in its misdeeds and have, thereby, justified its ways.

I hear many things about the RSS. I have heard it said that the RSS is at the root of all this mischief. Hinduism cannot be saved by orgies of murder. You are now a free people. You have to preserve your freedom. You can do so if you are humane and brave and ever-vigilant, or else a day will come when you will rue the folly which made this lovely prize slip from your hands.

* * *

General KM Cariappa of the Indian Army, in one of his utterances in England, had allowed himself to say that non-violence was of no use under the existing circumstances in India; only a strong army could make India one of the greatest nations in the world.

Gandhiji joined issue with him in *Harijan*: "Generals greater than General Cariappa have been wise and humble enough frankly to make the admission that they can have no right to speak of the possibilities of the great force of ahimsa. I make bold to say that in this age of the atom bomb, unadulterated non-violence is the only force that can confound all the tricks put together of violence. We are witnessing the tragic insolvency of military science and practice in its own home."

This in army language, as the General afterwards put it, was "a rocket"! But he took it sportingly. On his return to India he called on Gandhiji, on the eve of taking over the command of the Eastern Army. This was their first meeting. It was Gandhiji's day of silence. He was busy with his *charkha* (spinning wheel). Declining to take his seat on a chair that Gandhiji had offered him, the General respectfully sat on the floor.

"I have come here to receive your blessings," he said to Gandhiji.

The General smiled and said that he had seen it and had felt greatly honoured that the Mahatma should have taken the trouble to notice at length the views of a person like him, whom he had never met.

Coming to the point at issue, he said: "We, soldiers, are a very maligned community. Even you think that we are a very violent tribe. But we are not. Of all the peoples in this world, the one community which dislikes wars is the soldier community. It is not because of the dangers and horrors in the battlefield, but because of the knowledge we have of the utter futility of wars to settle international disputes. We feel one war merely leads to another. History has taught us this."

This testimony as to the utter futility of war as a means for settling international disputes from such an eminent professional soldier came to Gandhiji as an agreeable surprise. It made the search for an effective moral substitute for war common ground between them. This was half the battle won.

The General continued: "In a democratic country, soldiers do not initiate wars. Governments, when they have failed to get a satisfactory solution to international problems, declare wars. We merely carry out the orders of the Government and therefore, of the people. If people in a democracy do not like wars they should not blame us, but the Government they have put in power. It is quite simple for them, if they are not satisfied with the Government, to change the Government and put another in its place which will not resort to wars. So you see we are the innocent party. Why blame us?"

Gandhiji signalled to him to return the slip of paper he had given him. On it he again wrote: "When we meet again, I would like to further discuss this subject with you."

Two days later, they met again. Resuming their talk on non-violence, the General said: "I have come to tell you that we, soldiers, practise every bit of the ideologies which you practise, i.e. love and loyalty to mankind, discipline, selflessness in the service of our country, dignity of labour and non-violence. If we have to have an army at all, it must be a good one. I would like to remind them in my own way of the need for and the value of non-violence. I cannot possibly do my duty well by the country if I concentrate only on telling the troops of non-violence all the time, subordinating their main task of preparing themselves efficiently to be good soldiers. So I ask you, please, to give me the 'Child's Guide to Knowledge'. Tell me, please, how I can put the spirit of non-violence over to the troops without endangering their sense of duty to train themselves well professionally, as soldiers. I am a child in this matter. I want your guidance."

Gandhiji laughed. He was still at his *charkha*. He paused, looked at the General and said: "Yes you are all children; I am a child too, but I happen to be a bigger child than you because I have given more thought to this question than you all have."

Half closing his eyes, he stretched his right arm out to emphasize his words and added : "I am still groping in the dark for the answer. I will think about this seriously in the next few days and will let you know about it soon. However, I would like to see you more often, so that we may further discuss this important subject. I have always had the greatest admiration for the discipline in the army and also for the importance you army people pay to sanitation and hygiene. I tell my people to copy the army in these respects."

The General met Gandhiji for the last time on the 18th January, 1948. He had come to Delhi to take over the charge of the Western Command, which had the responsibility of conducting the operations in Jammu and Kashmir.

"I am going to Kashmir in a few days' time," he said.

"I hope you will succeed in solving the Kashmir problem non-violently," Gandhiji replied. "Come and see me after your return from Kashmir."

The General had been keenly looking forward to receiving in due course the 'Child's Guide to Knowledge'. It was a fascinating prospect —the General of India's non-violent struggle for freedom initiating the General of the Indian Army in the non-violent techniques and the two working together to discover an effective substitute for war, which they agreed settled nothing. Towards that object Gandhiji had collaborated with Badshah Khan and the fighting Pathans of the Frontier Province, that too with startling success!

But Providence had decreed otherwise. The General returned from Kashmir on the afternoon of the 30th January, 1948, to see the remains of Gandhiji at Rajghat the next day.

* * *

In the second week of December 1947, Gandhiji was having an argument with Shaheed Suhrawardy on the question of the recovery of abducted women from West Punjab. In the course of it, he said: "You must know that the people here and even in a greater measure the members of the Union Government do not have that trust in you that I have. They tell me that you are fooling me, that in Calcutta you hung on my words because the Muslims were in peril but here things are different and so are you. If you wish to remove their distrust and suspicion, you must have the courage to plainly tell Jinnah and Liaquat Ali that they must adopt a uniform policy with the Indian Union with regard to the recovery of the abducted women and other matters pertaining to the minorities. Similarly, you must ascertain the truth about what is said to be happening in Karachi and ask Jinnah how it comports with his declaration that the minorities in Pakistan would be fully protected. And if you cut no ice with them, you must, as a Muslim and an Indian national, issue a statement disapproving of Pakistan's policy in unequivocal terms. Thereby, you will serve both India and Pakistan."

This was the theme of many a discussion that Gandhiji had with Shaheed and with the local Muslims. In the grim battle that the Indian Union was fighting against the forces of communal fanaticism to make India safe for the minorities and ensure to them their full rights as Indian nationals, they had to courageously come out on the side of right and justice and speak out their mind to Pakistan.

* * *

I found Gandhiji to be the saddest man that one could picture when I rejoined him in mid-December, 1947. In the midst of the pomp and pageantry of the capital, surrounded by loving friends, and with his name on everybody's lips, he was spiritually isolated from his surroundings and from almost every one of his colleagues, who now held positions of power and prestige in the Government. The only political colleague of his who had remained unswerving in his loyalty to the creed of non-violence was Khan Abdul Ghaffar Khan, and it was him that the Congress decision to accept Partition had made a citizen of Pakistan.

By an almost superhuman effort of will Gandhiji was able, in the midst of all this, to preserve his balance and even his good humour. Everybody who came to him found him all attention, all serenity, all sweetness, full of the usual sunshine of his good humour. He seemed to have access to some hidden reservoir of strength, optimism, joy and peace, which was independent of outer circumstances and which was communicated to everybody who came in contact with him. Jawaharlal Nehru, Maulana Azad, Dr Rajendra Prasad and Sardar Patel—all of them seasoned soldiers and veteran fighters—came to him daily, often with grave, careworn faces, drawn looks, and heads bent under the load they carried. But within minutes of their arrival, Gandhiji's room would be ringing with loud peals of their laughter and when they left, it was with a light heart and a bright, joyous countenance, as if they had left all their cares and worries behind, with the unaging, perennially young old man whose spirit seemed to grow younger as he advanced in years.

* * *

Partition had left nearly 40 million Muslims in the Indian Union. The bulk of them had, under the Muslim League's propaganda, given their active or passive support to the division of India. The top Muslim League leaders had since migrated to Pakistan, leaving the rank and file of their co-religionists in a quandary—a confused, demoralized, leaderless mass, without a clearly defined policy or goal. Their emotional loyalty was still with the League. But the essential condition of their existence in the Indian Union as equal citizens was unreserved loyalty to the Indian Union. They all felt unhappy, bitterly disillusioned. Observed the leader of the Muslim League Party in the Orissa Assembly: "The Muslims of the Indian Union now realize that they have committed a blunder in supporting the movement for Pakistan."

The utterances of the leaders of Pakistan from across the border, their propaganda of exaggeration and hate against the Indian Union, and their lip-championship of the cause of the Indian Muslims did the Muslims little good, but needlessly deepened Hindu fears. The more sensible section among the Muslims saw this. The leader of the Muslim League Party in the Constituent Assembly of India, Khaliquzaman, was constrained to tell his erstwhile colleagues across the border to mind their own business and leave the Indian Muslims alone.

But the bulk of the pro-League section of the Muslims were sullen, when not actively disloyal. All this provided a fruitful soil for Hindu chauvinism. Its most serious manifestation was infiltration of the Hindu middle class and even the Government services by the RSS. It had even begun to command the secret sympathy of a section of Hindu Congressmen.

The RSS was a communalist, paramilitary, Fascist organization. Their declared object was to set up Hindu Raj. They had adopted the slogan, "Muslims, clear out of India". At the time, they were not very active, at least not overtly, but it was being darkly hinted that they were only waiting for all the Hindus and Sikhs in West Pakistan to be evacuated. They would then wreak full vengeance on the Indian Muslims for what Pakistan had done.

Gandhiji was determined not to be a living witness to such a tragedy. The Muslims were in a minority in the Indian Union. Why should they feel insecure as to their future as equal citizens in the Indian Union? It hurt him to see anyone live in fear, unable to walk with his head erect. Eager always to champion the cause of the underdog and to identify himself with the down and out, he set himself to put heart into the Indian Muslims. They had to be helped to reorganize themselves, rid themselves of the canker of divided loyalty and regain their integrity, dignity and self-respect, so that they might legitimately take pride in being the nationals of free India on an equal footing with the rest in every respect.

Thus, like a wise friend and guide, he missed no opportunity to restore to the Indian Muslims their lost fibre, while bringing home to them their errors which they had to live down and from the consequence of which there was no escape.

* * *

Many mosques in the capital had been damaged and occupied by the refugees during the disturbances. Some of them had been converted into temples by the refugees who had installed idols in them.

Gandhiji, in a note to Sardar Patel, had suggested that an announcement should be made that no sacrilege would be suffered in regard to mosques and if any damage occurred to them, repairs would be effected by the Government. Two days later, a communique was issued by the Delhi administration giving seven days' notice to the non-Muslims to vacate all mosques, failing which the police would eject them by force. The Government further decided to repair the damaged mosques.

This was good as far as it went. But Gandhiji said that, unless the idols were removed and mosques repaired by the Hindus themselves, he would not feel satisfied. Restitution of places of worship by the use of military or police force was a travesty—no restitution at all.

* * *

Quite a proportion of the police and military personnel in Delhi had their homes in West Punjab and the Frontier Province, now part of Pakistan. Some had been recruited from among the ranks of the refugees, as an emergency measure. A number of them had lost their near and dear ones. The relations of others had suffered indignities worse than death during the disturbances and they were now all thrown upon them as homeless destitutes, turning their homes into miniature refugee camps. Deep resentment and bitterness against the Muslims was the order of the day. The womenfolk, as might naturally be expected, were even more distraught and resentful than the men. The police did not openly defy the Government's orders. But very often they let their deep personal bitterness get the better of their sense of duty and discipline.

These were the agents through whom the administration had to be carried out. Sardar Patel was a very harassed man, and he was also very ill. The machine of which he was in charge could be run only in a particular way. He had to rely on his officers. They were his eyes and ears. He could not afford to lose their loyalty by putting too heavy a strain on it, or allow their morale to be affected in the difficult times through which they were passing. Gandhiji found himself in a very anomalous position. He did not want to do anything which might even have the appearance of intrusion or interference. He was treading on very thin ice. Everybody's nerves were on the edge. He had to be extremely cautious.

"People expect much from me," he observed at one of the prayer meetings, "but they must realize that I am not running the Government." Those at the helm of affairs were his friends, but he did not, he went on to say, want anyone to accept his advice merely out of friendship or regard for him. They should do so only if it went home to them.

* * *

Attempts to occupy Muslim houses continued. Again and again the police had to use tear gas. Gandhiji remarked that it was hard to lie in the open, in the biting cold of Delhi. When it rained, tents were not sufficient protection, but the squeezing out of the Muslims that was going on was both crooked and ungentlemanly. He could have understood their clamouring for houses, he said, if they had not made the Muslim houses their special target. They could have come to Birla House, turned him and the owners out and occupied the house. "That would be open dealing, though not gentlemanly." The fact that they insisted on occupying Muslim houses even though the authorities had offered them alternative accommodation clearly showed that it was not necessity that prompted them but the wish to get Delhi cleared of Muslims.

There were stresses and strains within the Cabinet too. Between Jawaharlal Nehru and Sardar Patel there was a difference in approach when it came to various questions. For instance, there was the RSS. Sardar Patel observed in one of his speeches: "In Congress there are some in power who feel that by virtue of authority they will be able to crush the RSS. You cannot crush an organization by using the rod. After all, RSS men are not thieves and dacoits. They are patriots, who love their country; only their trend of thought is misdirected."

It was an unfortunate utterance. Could the patriotic motive condone deeds in themselves heinous? Obviously, he had not foreseen what this softness would cost the country before long. When later, the RSS showed itself in its true colours, he was appalled and took prompt action—unfortunately, by then it was too late.

* * *

The Kashmir question had of late been becoming graver and graver with every passing day.

It was for the Indian Union, Gandhiji insisted, to do absolute justice even if heavens were to fall. In a conversation with a friend he let himself go, pouring forth for nearly three quarters of an hour the pent-up lava as he walked up and down his room in deep agitation. Let alone Kashmir, he said, he would not mind the loss of the whole of princely India if it could be retained only by the sacrifice of the principles for which the Indian Union stood—full justice and equal treatment to the minorities and punishment of the wrongdoers without fear or favour. An India reduced in size but purged in spirit might still take up the moral leadership of the world, bringing the message of hope and deliverance to the oppressed and exploited races. But an unwieldy, soulless India would merely be a third-rate imitation of the Western military states, utterly powerless to stand up against their onslaught.

The dying year closed for Gandhiji on a scene of unrelieved gloom, lit up only by his faith.

Taking stock, in a letter, of the situation around him, he wrote: "During the struggle against the British, we used to feel it was a hard fight; but today I find that it was a child's play compared with what confronts us today. We could then exaggerate—even make a mountain of a molehill—denouncing the British. But what is one to say today, now that we are applying the axe to our own feet? We turn away from the challenge of duty. There cannot be *surajya* (good government) unless we have effected self-purification. But Independence overtook us before we could do that. That is why we are where we are today."

Rajkumari Amrit Kaur brought a number of English friends one night to meet him. "No human being or religious institution is perfect in this imperfect world," he said to them in the course of the conversation. "Religious institutions are an answer to the challenge of the age and the particular circumstances prevailing at the time. Today we worship Christ, but the Christ in flesh, we crucified. Stoning prophets and erecting churches to their memory afterwards has been the way of the world through the ages. They, in the past, could at least plead in mitigation that they did not know what they were doing. We can offer no such defence. And as the Confucian saying goes: To know what is right and not to do it is cowardice."

Among those who came to offer New Year's greetings, was a visitor from Siam. He complimented Gandhiji on the independence that India had attained as a result of his labours. It had intensified the longing for freedom in all countries. Disclaiming the compliment, Gandhiji replied that what they in India had attained was in his eyes no independence at all. "Today, not everybody can move about freely in the capital. Indian fears his brother Indian. Is this independence?"

On the following day, he wrote: "Today, man fears man, neighbour distrusts neighbour. The metropolis of independent India looks like the City of the Dead. How strange that the peace of a country that won its independence through ahimsa is deemed to be safe only under the protection of *himsa* (violence)!"

On the 4th January, the Delhi maulanas came to see Gandhiji. They said to him: "We are in a predicament. We have no other support left besides you. We can no longer depend on the police." Gandhiji expressed deep sympathy with them. The police had become corrupt. It was deplorable. But while he was fighting their battle, he told his visitors, the nationalist Muslims had to do their part. If they used their influence to keep the mass of Indian Muslims on the right path in spite of all provocations, the Hindus and Sikhs were bound to come round in due course. Then, Pakistan was threatening war on India. They had to ponder well where their duty lay in that crisis. If they felt that Pakistan was in the wrong, they had to express their dissent publicly in clear and unequivocal terms.

A few days later, an esteemed woman worker and a very dear associate from Sind came and gave a harrowing description of the happenings there. Gandhiji's only comment was, how happier he would have been if instead of her coming to tell him all that, some one had given him the news that she had been killed in protecting the honour of Sindhi sisters! "The news from Sind has made me restless," he wrote in a letter. "I am anxious to visit Sind. But with what face can I go there? To rush forth to put out a conflagration elsewhere when your own house is burning is only to help spread the conflagration. In such circumstances, the best way to fight the conflagration elsewhere is to put out the fire in your own house and prevent it from spreading."

"I am in a furnace," he wrote in another letter. "There is a raging fire all around. We are trampling humanity under our feet."

His arrears of correspondence had been piling up. This worried him. So he discontinued having a nap after the morning prayer. "This is the only time when I can attend to my post," he wrote in one of his letters. "During the day, the non-stop stream of visitors leaves not a moment of free time."

But when it was suggested to him that it was time that he gave himself some rest, he brushed aside the suggestion saying what he needed was not rest but deliverance. "It is not the burden of work that weighs upon me."

On the 10th January, he said to his friends, the maulanas of Delhi who had come to him: "You have waited long enough. Have patience for yet another week and see what happens."

* * *

To the numerous causes of mounting tension between India and Pakistan was now added another—the issue of Pakistan's share of the cash balances of undivided India. Under the decision of the Partition Council, out of a total cash balance of 375 crore rupees, 20 crores were paid to Pakistan on the day of the transfer of power. The allocation was provisional and subject to readjustment that would have to be made when the balance was finally determined. This amount was subsequently fixed at 55 crore rupees after a series of conferences between the representatives of the two Dominions in the last week of November. The invasion of Kashmir by the raiders was in full swing at that point. Besides, there were several other issues. The Government of India, in the course of the negotiations, made it clear that it would not regard the settlement as final until agreement had been reached on all outstanding issues, and no payment would be made until the question of Kashmir was also settled. The Government of India was not prepared to provide Pakistan with the sinews of war to be used in its undeclared war against the Indian Union on the Kashmiri soil.

Gandhiji discussed the question with Lord Mountbatten and asked for his frank and candid opinion on the Government of India's decision. Mountbatten said, it would be the "first dishonourable act" by the Indian Union Government if the payment of the cash balance claimed by Pakistan was withheld. It set Gandhiji furiously thinking. He did not question the legality of the Indian Union's decision. Nor could he insist on the Union Government going beyond what the strict letter of the law required and permitted them. And yet, he felt it would be a tragedy if in a world dominated by the cult of expediency and force, the same India that had made history by winning her independence by predominantly non-violent, moral means, failed in that crisis to live up to her highest tradition that would serve as a shining beacon light to others.

Some maulanas of Delhi came to see Gandhiji on the 11th January. They were nationalist Muslims and had refused to go out of India, which they proudly claimed as their motherland. With great doggedness and courage, they had continued to stay on in Delhi even through the worst of times. But their patience, they complained to Gandhiji, was now nearly exhausted. One of them said to him: "How long do you expect the Muslims to put up with these pinpricks? If the Congress cannot guarantee their protection, let them plainly say so. The Muslims will then go away and be at least spared the daily insults and possible physical violence. For ourselves, we cannot even go to Pakistan, for as nationalist Muslims we have been opposed to its formation. On the other hand, Hindus will not allow us to live in the Indian Union either. Why not arrange a passage for us and send us to England, if you cannot guarantee our safety and self-respect here?"

"You call yourselves nationalist Muslims and you speak like this?" Gandhiji answered reproachfully. But the steely barb had entered into his heart. It was the last straw.

13

FROM THE DEPTH OF ANGUISH

On the 12th January in the afternoon, Gandhiji was sitting as usual, out on the sun-drenched spacious Birla House lawn. Since it was Monday, his day of weekly silence, he was writing out his prayer address. As my sister looked through sheet after sheet that she was to translate and read out to the prayer congregation in the evening, she was struck dumb. She came running to me with the news—Gandhiji had decided to launch on a fast unto death unless the madness in Delhi ceased.

From the time he had returned to Delhi, Gandhiji had never stopped asking himself where his duty lay in the face of what was happening. There was no answer he could give to the Muslims who came to him day after day and week after week with their tales of woe. He was impatient to go to the succour of the minority community in Sind and West Punjab, and to the Frontier Province to meet the Khan Brothers and their Khudai Khidmatgars, towards whom he felt a special responsibility, especially after Partition, apart from the common bond of non-violence that united them. But with what face or self-confidence could he go there when he could not guarantee full protection to the Delhi Muslims? He could not get the authorities to do more, and what they had succeeded in doing was in his eyes not enough. Perhaps, circumstanced as they were, they were not in a position to do more. He felt resourceless, and resourcelessness in the face of a moral challenge was something he could not stand. Out of the depth of his anguish came the decision to fast. It left no room for argument. Sardar Patel and Jawaharlal Nehru had been with him only a couple of hours before. He had given then no inkling of what was brewing within him.

The written address containing the decision was read out at the evening prayer meeting. The fast would begin on the next day after the midday meal. There would be no time limit. During the fast, he would take only water with or without salt and the juice of sour limes. The fast would be terminated only when and if he was satisfied that there was "a reunion of hearts of all the communities brought about without outside pressure but from an awakened sense of duty." The statement ran:

> One fasts for health's sake under laws governing health, or fasts as a penance for a wrong done and felt as such. There is, however, a fast which a votary of non-violence sometimes feels impelled to undertake by way of protest against some wrong done by society and this he does when he has no other remedy left. Such an occasion has come my way.
>
> When I returned to Delhi from Calcutta in September, gay Delhi looked like a city of the dead. At once I saw that I had to be in Delhi and "Do or Die". There is apparent calm brought about by prompt military and police action. But there is storm within the breast. It may burst forth any day.
>
> I never like to feel resourceless—a *satyagrahi* never should. My impotence has been gnawing at me of late. It will go immediately the fast is undertaken. I have been brooding over it for the last three days. The final conclusion has flashed upon me and it makes me happy. No man, if he is pure, has anything more precious to give than his life. I hope and pray that I have that purity in me to justify the step.

He asked all to bless his effort and to pray for him and with him. The statement continued:

> I flatter myself with the belief that India's loss of her soul will mean the loss of the hope of the aching, storm-tossed and hungry world. There are friends who do not believe in the method of the fast for the reclamation of the human mind. They will bear with

me and extend to me the same liberty of action that they claim for themselves. If I have made a mistake and discover it, I shall have no hesitation in proclaiming it from the house-tops and retracing my faulty steps.

A pure fast, like duty, is its own reward. I do not embark upon it for the sake of the result it may bring. I do so because I must. Hence, I urge everybody dispassionately to examine the purpose and let me die, if I must, in peace which I hope is ensured. Death for me would be a glorious deliverance, better than being a helpless witness to the destruction of India, Hinduism, Sikhism and Islam. That destruction is certain if Pakistan ensures no equality of status and security of life and property for all professing various faiths and if India copies her. Only then Islam dies in the two Indias, not in the world. But Hinduism and Sikhism have no world outside India.

The statement concluded with an entreaty:

Just contemplate the rot that has set in beloved India, and you will rejoice to think that there is a humble son of hers who is strong enough, and possibly pure enough, to take the happy step. If he is neither, he is a burden on earth. The sooner he disappears the better, for him and all concerned.

In reply to a question as to why he should have decided to launch on a fast at that juncture when "nothing extraordinary had happened", he answered that "death by inches" was far worse than sudden death. "It would have been foolish for me to wait till the last Muslim has been turned out of Delhi by subtle undemonstrative methods."

* * *

Devadas, Gandhiji's youngest son, made a thirteenth-hour attempt to dissuade him from the grave decision. Like everybody else, he had no inkling of what was coming. He learnt of the fast only after the decision had been announced. The next morning, he sent his father a note which he had written late at night. The note ran:

My chief concern and my argument against your fast is that you have surrendered to impatience, whereas your mission by its very nature calls for infinite patience. You do not seem to have realized what a tremendous success your patient labour has achieved. It has saved thousands of lives and may still save many more. By your death you will not be able to accomplish what you can by living. I would, therefore, beseech you to pay heed to my entreaty and give up your decision to fast.

This evoked from Gandhiji a reply that will live as an epic of faith. He did not agree that his decision to fast was hasty:

It was quick no doubt, so far as the drafting of the statement was concerned. Behind this lightning quickness was my four days' heart-churning and prayer. It cannot, therefore, be called hasty. Your worry as well as your pleading are equally vain. You are of course a friend, and a friend of a very high order at that. But you cannot get over the son in you. Your concern is natural and I respect it. But your argument betrays impatience and superficial thinking. I regard this step of mine as the acme of patience. Is patience which kills its very object patience or folly? And does it not betray sheer ignorance to attribute sudden loss of patience to one who has been patience personified since September last?

It was only when in terms of human effort I had exhausted all resources and realized my utter helplessness that I laid my head on God's lap. You would do well to read and ponder over *Gajendra Moksha*—the greatest of the devotional poems, as I have called it. Then alone, perhaps, you will be able to appreciate the step I have taken. Your last sentence is a charming token of your affection. But your affection is rooted in attachment or delusion. God sent this fast. He alone will end it, if and when He wills. In the meantime it behoves you, me and everybody to have faith that it is equally well whether He preserves my life or ends it, and to act accordingly. I can, therefore, only pray that He may lend strength to my spirit lest the desire to live may tempt me into premature termination of my fast.

The fast commenced with the singing of Gandhiji's favourite hymns, *Vaishnavajana* and *When I Survey the Wondrous Cross*.

With the launching of the fast, Gandhiji passed from tumult into peace. Those who had watched him closely since his return to the "City of the

Dead" in September testified that never had he appeared so cheerful and carefree as immediately after the commencement of his fast.

Neither Sardar Patel nor Jawaharlal Nehru tried to strive with him. A believer in deeds more than words, Sardar simply sent word that he would do anything that Gandhiji might wish. In reply, Gandhiji, suggested that the first priority should be given to the question of Pakistan's share of the cash assets.

Describing it as "my greatest fast", in a letter to Mirabehn he wrote: "Whether it will ultimately prove so or not, is neither your concern nor mine. Our concern is the act itself and not the result of action."

Maulana Azad had always shown an uncanny insight into Gandhiji's mind. He said: "Even if we were to dash our heads against a stone wall, his resolve once taken won't be given up. To argue further with him is only to prolong his agony. The only thing left for us is to begin thinking what we can do to fulfil his conditions which alone will induce him to give up his fast." And so they all set about to tackle the problem constructively.

At the evening prayer meeting, Gandhiji declared that he would break his fast only when conditions in Delhi permitted the withdrawal of the military and of the police without any danger to peace. The police might remain, but only to cope with anti-social elements, not to enforce communal peace.

Some people had complained that the Mahatma had sympathy only for the Muslims and had undertaken the fast for their sake. Gandhiji answered that in a sense they were right. All his life he had stood, as everyone should stand, for minorities or those in need. Pakistan had resulted in depriving the Muslims of India of their pride and self-confidence. It hurt him to think that this should be so. It weakened the foundations of a state to have any class of people lose self-confidence.

Though he had ceased to belong to any part of the country in an exclusive sense, Gujarat, his home province, had never ceased to be the mistress of his heart. As a Gujarati of Gujaratis, Gandhiji had a special claim upon them. They, to whom he had given of his best, had to represent the best that was in Gujarat and give to their common motherland their best. Had not Gujarat nearly three decades ago taken the lead which had launched India into the non-cooperation and finally, the Independence era? In the supreme crisis that was now upon him, his thoughts naturally turned to the men and women of Gujarat. On the second day of the fast, he sent them a message in the form of an open letter, "To the People of Gujarat". Though addressed primarily to Gujaratis, it was intended to speak to all the people of India:

I do not regard this as an ordinary fast. Behind it is the realization that there is a time for every thing, and an opportunity once missed never returns.

Delhi is the metropolis of India. If, therefore, we really do not, in our hearts, subscribe to the two-nation theory, in other words, if we do not regard the Hindus and the Muslims as constituting two distinct nations, we shall have to admit that the picture that Delhi presents today, is not what we have envisaged always of the capital of India. Delhi is the heart of India. From Kanya Kumari to Kashmir and from Karachi to Dibrugarh in Assam, all Hindus, Muslims, Sikhs, Parsis, Christians and Jews who people this vast sub-continent and have adopted it as their dear motherland, have an equal right to it. No one can say that it belongs to the majority community only and that the minority community can only remain there as the underdog. Therefore, anyone who wants to drive all Musalmans out of Delhi, must be set down as its enemy number one and therefore enemy number one of India. We are rushing towards that catastrophe. It is the bounden duty of every son and daughter of India to take his or her full share in averting it.

What shall we do, then? If we are to see our dream of *Panchayat Raj* (true democracy) realized, we should regard the humblest and lowest Indian as being equally the ruler of India as the tallest in the land. No one would then harbour any distinction between community and community. No one would regard another as untouchable. We would hold as equal the toiling labourer and the rich capitalist. Everybody would know how to earn an honest living by the sweat of his brow and make no distinction between intellectual and physical labour.

At the evening prayer meeting, he drew a glowing picture of what would happen if there was a wave of self-purification all over India:

Before I ever knew anything of politics in my early youth, I dreamt the dream of communal unity of the heart. I shall jump like a child, in the evening of my life, to feel that the dream has been realized in this life. Who would not risk sacrificing his life for the realization of such a dream?

* * *

Within 24 hours of the commencement of the fast, the Cabinet of the Indian Union met on the lawn of Birla House around Gandhiji's fasting bed to consider afresh the issue of Pakistan's share of the cash balances. But it made angrier still those who were already angry with Gandhiji for what they considered as his partiality towards the Muslims. A fanatical group among them began to organize a dark conspiracy to compass his death.

At night, some Sikhs from West Punjab held a demonstration in front of Birla House, shouting, "Blood for blood", "We want revenge", "Let Gandhi die". Jawaharlal Nehru had just boarded his car to leave Birla House after meeting Gandhiji. On hearing the shouts he got down from the car and rushed out. "Who dares to shout 'Let Gandhi die'?" he roared. "Let he who dares repeat those words in my presence. He will have to kill me first." The demonstrators scurried away helter-skelter.

Inside his darkened room, Gandhiji lay in his bed. Hearing the noise outside, he asked: "What are they shouting?"

"They are shouting, 'Let Gandhi die'."

With a sigh he began to recite the *Ramanama*.

"Bapu, during your Calcutta fast you were very cheerful and even cracked jokes with us, but you look very grave now," someone remarked. Gandhiji replied: "Yes, it was comparatively easy-going in Calcutta. The task here is far more difficult. There was no refugee problem there to complicate the issue."

The news about Gandhiji's fast set up a deep "heart searching" among all sections. Leaders not only in India but also in Pakistan began to ask themselves what had led Gandhiji to take such an extreme step; whether by indulging in senseless vendetta, they were not really ill-serving their religion and driving their respective countries to suicide. It steadied the waverers and lent courage and strength to those who, from sluggishness or timidity had hitherto indecisively hung back, instead of coming out fearlessly to denounce the misdeeds of their co-religionists. This applied particularly to the Indian Muslims.

A stream of messages of sympathy and support poured in from Muslim leaders and Muslim organizations all over India and even from abroad. Dr Zakir Husain, the chief of the Muslim National University, Delhi, wrote:

> We have no doubt that you are guided by a superior wisdom, and that you have chosen the right moment to urge your people to purify their hearts. God has given you strength and a confidence which does not fail and a faith that adverse circumstances cannot shake. God is with you and you must succeed. Only we are overwhelmed with shame that free India should have nothing to offer you but bitterness and distress. May God spare you to lead us onward towards the higher freedom for which you have been striving, and of which, in spite of all our blindness and misdeeds, you still believe us worthy. If anything can transform us, it is your faith that the highest in us must and will assert itself.

Of particular significance was an injunction by a Muslim divine from Bareilly to his followers:

> There is no greater friend of Musalmans than you, whether in Pakistan or Hindustan. My heart bleeds with yours at the recent Karachi and Gujarat (Pakistan) atrocities, the massacre of innocent men, women and children, forcible conversion and the abduction of women. These are crimes against Allah for which there is no pardon. Let the Pakistan Government know that. Much less can an Islamic State be founded upon such heinous crimes against Allah's creation. I order my followers in Pakistan and appeal to the Pakistan Muslims and Government to put an end to these shameful, un-Islamic misdeeds and express unqualified repentance. My order to my followers and to the Muslims of Hindustan is (that) they must remain loyal to the Union Government to the last and condemn the misdeeds of their co-religionists in Pakistan in emphatic terms to create public abhorrence against such action. It is high time that Musalmans should realize that their sincere loyalty to the Union and their leaders' confidence in

themselves are the only safeguards that can protect them. The secret desire to look to Pakistan for guidance and help will be their doom. Pray break your fast and save Hindustan and Pakistan from ruin, disaster and death.

Ever since the Great Calcutta Killing of August 1946, Gandhiji had been telling Muslims that if they continued to sit on the fence instead of courageously denouncing the excesses of their co-religionists, if they failed to align themselves with the victims of the same even at the risk of their lives, or if they harboured secret sympathies with the perpetrators of those excesses, it would bring down upon them the wrath of those with whom—Pakistan or no Pakistan—the bulk of them had to live. But his warning had largely fallen upon unheeding ears, with the unfortunate result that the Indian Muslims, having allowed the proverbial wind to be sown, were now faced with the prospect of having to reap the whirlwind. At the commencement of his fast he had told a group of maulanas, who came to request him to reverse his decision, that if happenings like the recent massacre of the Hindu and Sikh refugees on the train at Gujarat continued unchecked, "even ten Gandhis would not be able to save the Indian Muslims."

The statement from Bareilly was therefore a very welcome portent of a change which all his efforts before the fast had failed to achieve. He reinforced that appeal in the course of his prayer address with a few straight words of his own. "It is impossible to save the lives of the Muslims in the Union," he warned, "if the Muslim majority in Pakistan do not behave as decent men and women."

The response of Pakistan to Gandhiji's fast exceeded everybody's expectation. In the twinkling of an eye, the Muslim League's enemy number one of pre-Partition days was transfigured into their "greatest friend", and became the object of their anxious concern. Moving references to Gandhiji's fast were made in the course of their speeches by the members, on the floor of the West Punjab (Pakistan) Assembly. "No country in the world has produced a greater man, religious founders apart, than Mahatma Gandhi," remarked Malik Feroz Khan Noon of "outdoing Chengiz Khan" fame.

* * *

On the third day of his fast, Gandhiji felt distinctly weaker and had to be taken to the bathroom in a chair. A medical bulletin issued in the evening ran: "He is naturally losing weight, the weakness has increased. The voice is feeble. Acetone bodies have appeared in the urine." This meant, the bulletin went on to explain, he had entered what in medical language they call the "danger zone".

In one of his prayer addresses, Gandhiji had said something about the Muslim League being responsible for much that had happened in both parts of India. It brought from Shuaib Qureshi, a close friend of Gandhiji, a letter of protest. But Gandhiji felt that he had now earned the right to call a spade a spade and to administer wholesome advice, no matter how unpalatable it was to all Muslims and even to Pakistan. He asked me to write to Shuaib that he was unrepentant for what he had said about the Muslim League's responsibility for the existing state of affairs:

> I cannot, in all honesty, absolve it. Nor must I in this crisis mince words or keep back things which might displease others. It is the privilege of friendship to speak out the truth even though it might sound unpleasant to the ear, in the hope that genuine friendship will survive all jars.

Gandhiji went on to say:

> My fast, as I have stated in plain language, is undoubtedly on behalf of the Muslim minority in the Union, and therefore it is necessarily against the Hindus and the Sikhs of the Union and the Muslims of Pakistan. It is also on behalf of the minorities in Pakistan as of the Muslim minority in the Union.

On the third day of Gandhiji's fast, the Government of India announced that it had decided to pay Pakistan immediately the sum of 55 crore rupees. The communique went on to say:

> The Government have shared the world-wide anxiety over the fast undertaken by the Father of the Nation. In common with him they have anxiously searched for ways and means to bury the hatchet of ill-will, prejudice and suspicion, which has poisoned the relations of India and Pakistan.

Characterizing the Union Government's decision as a "unique action", Gandhiji observed: "It is never a light matter for any responsible Cabinet to alter a deliberate, settled policy. Yet our Cabinet, responsible in every sense of the term, has with equal deliberation yet promptness unsettled their settled fact. I know that all the nations of the earth will proclaim this gesture as one which only a large-hearted Cabinet could rise to."

But so far as the question of the breaking of the fast was concerned, he was still adamant. The doctors felt deeply worried over the failing kidney function. They dreaded not so much an instantaneous collapse as the permanent after-effects of any further prolongation. But Gandhiji told them, "I dread neither death nor permanent injury. But I do feel that the warning of the medical friends should—if the country has any use for me—hurry the people to close their ranks. Like brave men and women that we ought to be under hard-won freedom, we should trust even those whom we may suspect to be our enemies. Brave people disdain distrust."

This last was in answer to the fears of those who were opposed to the release of Rs 55 crores to Pakistan, lest it should be used to sustain the military aggression against Kashmir. Gandhiji had not a shadow of doubt that in the balance, India would gain by it.

* * *

Sardar Patel had to leave for Saurashtra on the 16th January for an important engagement. Gandhiji had insisted on his keeping it. Before leaving, he addressed a letter to Gandhiji:

I have to leave for Kathiawad at 7 this morning. It is agonizing beyond endurance to have to go away when you are fasting. But stern duty leaves no other course.

On returning to Bombay from Saurashtra, the Sardar unburdened himself in a public speech: "If, in spite of having achieved Independence, Gandhiji has to fast in order to achieve real Hindu-Muslim unity, it is a standing shame to us. You have just now heard people shouting that Muslims should be removed from India. Those who do so have gone mad with anger. Even a lunatic is better than a person who is mad with rage. He can be treated and perhaps cured, but the other? They do not realize that they stand to gain nothing by driving out a handful of Muslims. I am a frank man. I say bitter things to Hindus and Muslims alike. Some of them (Muslims) went to Gandhiji and complained about my Lucknow speech in which I had criticized them for not condemning Pakistan's attitude on Kashmir. Gandhiji felt compelled to defend me. That pained me. For I am not a weak person who should be defended by others."

* * *

Persistent refusal on Gandhiji's part to terminate the fast led everybody to ask what specific test would satisfy him. Just then arrived a telegram from Karachi. Muslim refugees who had been driven out of Delhi asked whether they could now return to Delhi and reoccupy their original houses. "That is the test!" Gandhiji remarked, as soon as he had read the telegram.

I immediately set out with that telegram on a round of all the Hindu and Sikh refugee camps in the city to explain to them what they had to do to enable Gandhiji to end his fast. By night, 1000 refugees had signed a declaration that they would welcome the Muslims to return and occupy their original homes even though with their families, they might have themselves to weather the biting winter cold of Delhi in refugee camps. Some refugees who were settled in the houses of Muslims said they would vacate them to make room for the returning owners: "We give you our fullest assurance that we shall welcome the return of Muslims to their homes in Delhi from any part of Pakistan. We shall work for making India as much a home for Muslims as it is for Hindus, Sikhs and other communities of India. Pray break your fast to save India from misery."

The Delhi administration announced that within a week's time, every non-Muslim refugee in Delhi would be provided with some kind of shelter. Jawaharlal Nehru and some Ministers of the Central Cabinet threw open their official residences to all homeless refugees, short of moving out themselves.

Then, as had so often happened before, the tide began to turn fast. There were numerous processions parading through various parts of the city shouting unity slogans and praying for the long life of the Mahatma.

* * *

The Nawab of Maler Kotla narrated to Gandhiji how during the disturbances, when some of the Muslim refugees in his State had begun to threaten the local Sikhs, he announced that for every Sikh or Hindu molested, he would shoot ten Muslims. "Not a single incident occurred after that." One of his ancestors, he narrated, had courageously stood up against Emperor Aurangzeb when the latter had declared his intention of killing the sons of one of the Sikh Gurus. Since then, the Sikhs everywhere had given asylum to the Muslims from Maler Kotla and vice versa. As a result, during the post-Partition communal troubles, Maler Kotla became a sanctuary for Sikhs and Hindus. Similarly, it was reported that, when Muslims travelling anywhere in the Punjab could prove that they were from Maler Kotla, they were given protection by the Sikhs. When Gandhiji heard this, he exclaimed, "So my dream for India came true in Maler Kotla!"

* * *

Arthur Moore, veteran journalist and former editor of *The Statesman,* had all along been a sceptic as to the validity of the method of fasting for solving social problems. But a change had been coming over him since Gandhiji's Calcutta fast, in August, 1947. He started fasting in sympathy when he heard about Gandhiji's decision to fast for communal peace in the capital. In a note which he addressed to Gandhiji, he wrote:

I am not one of those who would seek to dissuade you. I am sure you are right. Only a miracle can save the two Dominions from further terrible disasters if these hatreds continue. You did much in Calcutta. But far more is needed here; you are the only hope. I feel that people who approve and sympathize can help and strengthen you by fasting in sympathy. For this reason I also have not tasted food or any liquor but water since you began your fast, and I hope to continue while you fast. Last night, I fulfilled a dinner engagement but joined only in the conversation. I think you will, this time, change many hearts. You can be sure you have my prayers.

Gandhiji was deeply touched. He dictated a reply: "He believes you will do better work by moving about and mixing with the people and influencing them. He would, therefore, urge you to give up the fast, unless there is an imperative spiritual call."

Towards evening, on the 17th January, nausea set in and the heaviness in Gandhiji's head increased.

Nehru, as he looked at the suffering form before him, could bear the agony of it no longer. Quickly he turned away his face to wipe from his eye a glistening tear.

An astonishing thing about Gandhiji's long fasts was the phenomenal mental vigour and energy that he exhibited during them. The mind became more keen and alert as the fast progressed, the intuitions sharper, the insight deeper and the spirit more sensitive, and full of forgiveness and compassion. The schedule on the fifth day of his fast was as follows:

The morning prayer as usual at 3.30 am; after his daily Bengali writing, he had the morning papers and important incoming letters and telegrams read out to him; medical check-up by the doctors followed by massage and bath etc till 10.30 am; dictated to me his statement on the Government of India's decision on the release of Pakistan's share of the cash balances while lying in his bathtub. Between 10.30 am and midday, received seven visitors, including three ruling Chiefs of States. Between 12.30 and 3.35 pm, in between rest and various items of nature-cure treatment, again had serious talks with ten visitors, including Jawaharlal Nehru, Maulana Azad and four maulanas of Delhi. After the evening prayer, received a big crowd of people.

The doctors' bulletin on the fifth day of the fast sounded a grave note of warning: "It is our duty to tell the people to take immediate steps to produce the requisite conditions for ending the fast without delay."

Addressing a peace rally in the city the same evening, Maulana Azad informed the gathering that he had met Gandhiji in the afternoon and told him that while he had undertaken the fast to bring about "a change of heart" among the people, it was difficult to assess when the required change of heart had taken place. Could not Gandhiji, therefore, let them have concrete conditions which, if fulfilled, would persuade him to break his fast? Gandhiji had thereupon mentioned to him seven conditions. The fast would be ended when all parties gave their signatures to those conditions. The assurances, Gandhiji had further said, had to come from responsible people, who could guarantee their proper fulfilment. The Maulana warned: "To that apostle of Truth we must give true assurance only. We are not to concoct make-believes even to save his life. If we can perform what he has called upon us to do, then alone can we go to him and ask him to give up his fast."

As a mark of popular concern, all business in the city was suspended for the day and Muslims, Hindus and Sikhs in their thousands came out and formed mixed processions. One of them was nearly one hundred thousand—strong and over a mile long. They all converged on Birla House, and dispersed.

A Central Peace Committee, consisting of 130 members representing all communities, was formed under the Chairmanship of Dr Rajendra Prasad, the Congress President. The Committee adopted a resolution assuring Gandhiji that they would do all that lay in their power, "to create, establish and maintain the spirit of peace, harmony and brotherhood between all communities." The representatives of some Hindu organizations, noted for their extreme communal bias, were not present in this meeting.

The Peace Committee met again on the morning of the 18th January. The absentees of the previous night were present. The representatives of all the important groups and organizations in the city were there, including representatives of the refugees from the worst affected parts. They all accepted the conditions laid down by Gandhiji and signed the following pledge:

We wish to announce that it is our heartfelt desire that Hindus, Muslims, Sikhs and members of other communities should once again live in Delhi like brothers and in perfect amity. We take the pledge that we shall protect the life, property and faith of the Muslims and that the incidents which have taken place in Delhi will not happen again.

1. We want to assure Gandhiji that the annual fair at Khwaja Qutabuddin's Mausoleum will be held this year as in previous years.

2. The Muslims will be able to move about just as they could in the past.

3. The mosques, which have been left by the Muslims and which are now in the possession of Hindus and Sikhs will be returned.

4. We shall not object to the return to Delhi of the Muslims who have migrated from here and the Muslims shall be able to carry on their business as before. We give the assurance that all these things will be done by our personal efforts and not with the help of the police or the military.

We request Mahatmaji to believe us and give up his fast and continue to lead us as he has done hitherto.

All the committee members arrived at Birla House. The gathering included Jawaharlal Nehru and Maulana Azad, Zahid Husain, the High Commissioner for Pakistan, and representatives of the Delhi Muslims, the RSS, the Hindu Mahasabha and various Sikh organizations.

In view of the guarantees that had jointly and severally been given, Dr Rajendra Prasad proceeded, they all hoped that Gandhiji would now break his fast.

Replying, Gandhiji said that they had given him all that he had asked for. But he reminded them that he was not a man to shirk another fast, if he afterwards discovered that he had been deceived into breaking it prematurely. They should, therefore, be extremely wary and act with full sincerity. He invited the representatives of Muslims who had been meeting him frequently to tell him whether they were satisfied that the conditions in Delhi were now such as to warrant his breaking the fast.

Concluding, Gandhiji remarked that if they fully accepted the implications of their pledge, they should release him from Delhi so that he might be free to go to Pakistan. In his absence, they should welcome such refugees from Pakistan as might want to return to their homes.

After the High Commissioner for Pakistan had reiterated the appeal, followed by the representatives of the Hindu Mahasabha, the RSS, the Sikhs and the representative of the Delhi Administration, Gandhiji broke the fast by receiving the glass of orange juice at the hands of Maulana Azad. Jawaharlal Nehru's eyes were wet with tears.

The gathering then dispersed, but Nehru stayed on. It was only then that he revealed to Gandhiji that he had been fasting with him from the day before. He had kept it as a closely guarded secret even from members of his own household. Gandhiji was deeply moved. As soon as Nehru had left, he scribbled a note and gave it to me to be delivered to him personally. The note read: "Now break your fast. May you live for many long years and continue to be the Jawahar (the jewel) of India. Bapu's blessings."

In the midst of it all, Gandhiji suddenly remembered Arthur Moore. "Telephone to Moore at once," he said to my sister, "that I have broken my fast and that he should now break his. And give him instructions as to the proper way of breaking a fast. This probably being his first fast, he might not be aware of the correct way." On being contacted over the phone, Arthur Moore, however, replied that he had already, on receiving the happy news a little while ago, broken his fast with a cup of coffee and a cigar!

In many camps, the refugees had started fasting with Gandhiji. They said they would break their fast only after Gandhiji had broken his. At noon, on the 18th January, about 100 Muslim women in purdah came to Birla House. Although the doctors had interdicted all visits, Gandhiji asked them to be brought into his presence. They said that for the last five days they had been fasting and praying in their homes that God might spare him. "You do not observe purdah before your fathers and brothers, then why do you observe it in my presence?" Gandhiji asked them. Up went the purdah. "It is not the first time that the purdah has disappeared before me," Gandhiji remarked afterwards. "This shows what genuine love can do."

Gandhiji's fasts touched the hearts of the millions in India because by ceaseless striving he had so completely identified himself with those millions, he had made their joys and sufferings his own to such an extent that when he suffered, they suffered with him.

14

THE DROP MERGES WITH THE OCEAN

Once more the battleship had gone into action and come out with the colours unsoiled, but with the hull this time badly damaged. In a letter to a close Ashram associate, a few days later, Gandhiji wrote: "My strength is fairly returning but the kidney and the liver seem to have been damaged this time."

But he had come out of such experiences and upset textbook medical theories often enough before. Thanks to his regular habits, abstemious living, self-discipline, detachment and poise, his system still retained its ample recuperative powers; the body was extremely well preserved, wiry and resilient; the various faculties and organs intact and functioning to perfection. There was absolute command over sleep. "When I lose command over sleep," he used to say, "I shall be finished. It will be a sign not merely of physical decay but of the deterioration of the spirit as well." Memory betrayed at times signs of flagging but the mind was razor-sharp, vigorous and quick; the judgment uncannily sure, and the intuitions, if anything, more unerring than ever. For all his age, he could still put in an amazing amount of physical and sustained, concentrated mental work. He was at the height of his spiritual powers. Never had his prestige at home and abroad stood higher.

* * *

Gandhiji's convalescence after the fast ran a smooth, uneventful course. He lost no time in taking up the loose ends of the various problems that he had been tackling before he launched on to the fast. They were the recovery of the abducted women in both the dominions to the tune of several thousands, the treatment of the Hindu population of Sind and the evacuation of those who wanted to come away.

In the meantime, two Parsi friends, who had on their own been trying to explore avenues to peace and goodwill between the two dominions, had returned from Karachi on the 19th January, after a series of talks with the Pakistan authorities.

The Parsi friends from Karachi argued that if he went to Pakistan, it would encourage the minority community there. Gandhiji, too, felt that having done his bit for the minority community in the Indian Union he had to now do the same for the minority community in Pakistan, and the way had now been set clear for him. The Delhi Muslims pressed the view that if the Hindus in the Indian Union knew that Gandhiji was going to Pakistan to help the minority community there, it would give impetus to the implementation of the peace effort that had been launched in Delhi.

After considering the various pros and cons, Gandhiji finally told the Parsi friends that he would go to Pakistan if the Pakistan authorities invited him. He would go to Sind on the invitation of the Chief Minister of Sind, who was known to be desirous of his visit there. He would then go to the Frontier Province. Something within him kept telling him that if he went to Pakistan and let the Muslim masses see in his face and in his eyes and in his whole being the love that made no distinction between Hindu and Muslim and which had made him offer his life as ransom to make India safe for Muslims, it might bring home to them the error and futility of divisiveness and, if it pleased God, He might use him to perform yet another miracle of conversion such as Calcutta and Delhi had witnessed. A Muslim leader from Pakistan came and told him that he looked forward to witnessing a fifty-mile long procession of Hindus and Sikhs returning to Pakistan with Gandhiji at its head. He had been working towards that end by his uncompromising insistence on its counterpart, the return and rehabilitation of the displaced Indian Muslims in their original homes. The tide of history would have then, at least so far as India was concerned, run a different course. And who could tell with what results? The prospect thrilled Gandhiji.

* * *

The last week of January 1948, and the last in Gandhiji's life, was crowded with momentous utterances.

On the 27th, he set out to attend the annual Urs (death anniversary) at Mehrauli. Set in the midst of idyllic surroundings, seven miles south of Delhi is Mehrauli, famed in history as the ancient capital of Prithviraj. It is the seat of the Dargah Sharif of Khwaja Syed Qutubuddin Bakhtiar —a shrine ranking second in holiness and sanctity only to the world famous *dargah* (a shrine built over the grave of a revered religious figure) of Khwaja Mohayuddin Chishti at Ajmer. During the disturbances, it had witnessed some ghastly deeds. A great religious fair was held there every year, attended not only by Muslims from all over India but even by Hindus—such is the catholicity and tradition of religious tolerance for which Sufism stands. Owing to disturbed conditions, it was feared that the fair might not be held that year. But Gandhiji had made the holding of the fair one of the conditions for breaking his fast and all parties had pledged themselves to its fulfillment. The Delhi Administration had got the precincts of the shrine and its environ cleaned up and the damage which the shrine had suffered during the disturbances, repaired as far as possible. *Sanatani* (traditional orthodox) Hindus and militant Sikhs vied with each other in fraternizing with the Muslims. They welcomed them with flowers and opened for them free tea-stalls. It was a sight to see Hindu and Sikh volunteers stand shoulder to shoulder with Muslim volunteers to render social service. No one could have imagined a few days earlier that such a vast fraternal crowd of Hindus, Muslims and Sikhs of Delhi could assemble there like that to celebrate a Muslim festival. Most agreeably surprising was the presence of hundreds of Hindu and Sikh women in the crowd. The atmosphere was redolent of the days of Hindu-Muslim unity.

"I am afraid Hindu and Sikh shrines in Pakistan must have suffered similar damages," Gandhiji remarked with a deep sigh as he saw the marks of vandalism on the lovely marble screen in the *dargah*.

According to a statement issued by the Pakistan Government, 130 innocent Hindus and Sikhs had been killed in the Parachinar refugee camp, at Peshawar by raiders from across the tribal territory. The actual casualties, it was feared, were many more. And yet, the news had not provoked any outbreak of violence in the capital. "I must say," remarked Gandhiji as he came out of the shrine, "the response of the Sikhs to my call to non-violent courage has exceeded my expectations."

* * *

The whole day on the 29th January was crammed with engagements. At the end of it he felt utterly exhausted. "My head is reeling. And yet I must finish this," he remarked to Abha, pointing to the draft of the Congress constitution, which he had undertaken to prepare.

Surveying the political scene, he mused why Congressmen, who had toiled and sacrificed for freedom's sake and on whom now rested the burden of independence, were succumbing to the lure of office and power. "Where will this take us?" And then, in a tone of infinite sadness, he repeated the well-known verse of Nazir, the celebrated Urdu poet of Allahabad:

Short-lived is the splendour of Spring, in the garden of the world,
Watch the brave show while it lasts.

Presently, he had a severe fit of coughing. To one of his attendants who was massaging his head, he said: "If I die of a lingering illness, nay even by as much as a boil or a pimple, it will be your duty to proclaim to the world, even at the risk of making people angry with you, that I was not the man of God that I claimed to be. If you do that, it will give my spirit peace. Note down this also that if someone were to end my life by putting a bullet through me—as someone tried to do with a bomb the other day—and I met his bullet without a groan, and breathed my last taking God's name, then alone would I have made good my claim."

* * *

On the fateful day of Friday, the 30th January, 1948, Gandhiji woke up as usual at 3.30 am. After the morning prayer, he sat down on his pallet to complete the draft of his note on the reorganization of the Congress which he had been unable to finish on the previous night.

He was still feeling weak after his fast. He did not feel well enough to go out for his morning walk. So he paced up and down for a while inside his room. He used to take palm-jaggery lozenges with powdered cloves to allay his cough. The clove powder had run out. Manu, therefore, instead of joining him in his constitutional, sat down to prepare some. "I shall join you presently," she said to him, "otherwise, there will be nothing at hand at night when it is needed." Gandhiji did not like anyone missing his duty in the immediate present to anticipate and provide for the uncertain future. "Who knows what is going to happen before nightfall or even whether I shall be alive?" he said to Manu and then added: "If at night I am still alive you can easily prepare some then."

Passing through my room for his massage at the usual time, he handed me the draft of the new constitution for the Congress—his Last Will and Testament to the nation—and asked me to go through it carefully.

He then had his bath. Coming out after his bath, he looked much refreshed. The strain of the previous night had disappeared and he was full of his usual sunlit humour.

After doing his daily exercise in Bengali writing, he had his morning meal. At half past ten, he laid himself down on his cot for rest, doing his daily Bengali reading before he dozed off. At 1.30 in the afternoon he had his abdominal mud pack. The sun was warm. So he slipped on his Noakhali peasants bamboo hat to shade his face.

* * *

Returning from the city, I went straight to the prayer ground. I had hardly reached the colonnade of stones that leads to the prayer ground when BP Chandwani, one of Gandhiji's aids, came running down from the opposite direction. "Telephone for a doctor at once," he shouted. "Bapu has been shot dead!"

I stood petrified as in a nightmare. What was there to telephone for if Bapu was "shot dead?" Mechanically, I asked someone to ring for a doctor.

The still, limp body was carried inside by friends. Gently, they laid him on the mattress where he used to sit and work. But before anything could be done, the clock had ceased to tick.

First to arrive at Birla House from among Gandhiji's colleagues was Sardar Patel. He sat down by his side, felt the pulse and fancied it was still beating feebly. Dr Bhargava examined the pulse and the eye reflexes a little later and slowly muttered, "Dead for ten minutes." By the side of the Mahatma's lifeless body sat Sardar Patel with his wan, haggard face set like granite. Next came Jawaharlal Nehru who, burying his face in Gandhiji's clothes, sobbed like a child. Devadas, the Mahatma's youngest son, followed and tenderly taking his father's hand into his, burst into tears.

Sardar Patel felt crushed. "Others can weep and find relief from their grief in tears," he remarked to me afterwards. "I cannot do that. But it reduces my brain to pulp."

In an adjoining low-lit room sat Nehru in a chair, deeply exercised over arrangements to be made for the funeral procession and the cremation ceremony on the next day. He narrated afterwards: "Suddenly I said to myself, let me go and consult Bapu. Then I realized! So accustomed has the mind become to taking all our difficulties to him."

As I gazed at the still, sad face, infinite peace, forgiveness, and compassion writ large on it, the entire vista of 28 long years of close, unbroken association from the time when, fresh from the college, I had come to him, full of dazzling dreams and undimmed hopes, and sat at his feet, flashed across the mind's eye. And what crowded years at that!

* * *

The funeral procession was about to start when, suddenly, there was a stir near the gate. Sushila had just arrived from Lahore.

She was at Multan (West Punjab) on the 30th January, on her way back to Delhi. "When is Gandhiji coming to us," asked the wife of the Deputy Commissioner, who had invited her for a cup of tea. Minutes later, another woman dashed into the room in great agitation, exclaiming, "What is the world coming to? They say Gandhiji is shot!"

Narrated Sushila afterwards: "I turned pale and began to shiver, saying to myself: No, no, it must be only a rumour."

"We shall ring up Delhi and find out," the Deputy Commissioner said. But Sushila did not want to find out. She wanted to cling to the last thread of hope. The wound might not be serious after all. "Please don't," she answered. "Let me proceed to Lahore immediately. I want to reach Delhi as soon as possible."

The Deputy Commissioner lent his car to take her to Lahore. After an all-night drive, the car reached Lahore at 6 am. A friend came to sympathize. Her manner frightened Sushila. A little later, Jawaharlal Nehru's familiar voice was heard on the radio. His broadcast address of the previous evening was being relayed. It left no room for hope. She was stunned. It seemed an endless wait before the plane took off.

On board the plane with her was Mian Iftekharuddin, a Muslim leader of West Punjab. He had rushed impulsively to Delhi to have Gandhiji's last *darshan*. As they alighted from the plane, Mian Saheb said to her in a choked voice: "My dear sister, the man who pulled the trigger is not Bapu's murderer. All of us who at any time doubted his word and entertained a feeling of violence and communalism in our hearts are responsible for his murder."

"Why this punishment!" Sushila exclaimed in anguish that evening, still disconsolate at not having been able to be by Gandhiji at the last moment. Devadas consoled her: "It was no punishment; it was your proud privilege to be executing Bapu's last order. You are luckier by far than any of us."

In those difficult days, when the ship of India's independence was labouring over the harbour bar in the rough seas around, one often heard the exclamation: "What would we not give to have him back with us for even one short hour to guide and advise us?" This was but natural. But sometimes one wondered.

> Do we indeed desire the dead
> Should still be near us at our side?
> Is there no baseness we would hide?
> No inner vileness that we dread?
> How pure at heart and sound in head,
> With what divine affections bold,

180

Should be the man whose thought would hold
An hour's communion with the dead.

* * *

Many friends would have liked a part of the *asthis* (ashes) to be preserved and kept in a public place after the manner of the Buddha's sacred relics. Some of his closest associates asked to be permitted personally to retain a part of the remains as a token. In view of Gandhiji's repeated injunction in the matter, however, it was decided not to allow any departure from what was known to be his specific wish. He had long ceased to belong to his family. No individual by virtue of blood or any other personal tie had a special claim upon him. Home he had none, or rather the whole world was his home, and mankind his family. What could not be shared with the least, he held to be of little account and not worth having. He summed up the whole philosophy of his life thus:

I recognize no God except that God that is to be found in the hearts of the dumb millions. And I worship the God that is Truth through the service of these millions. I believe in the absolute oneness of God and, therefore, of humanity. What though we have many bodies? We have but one soul. The rays of the sun are many through refraction. But they have the same source. I cannot, therefore, detach myself from the wickedest soul, nor may I be denied identity with the most virtuous.

With that philosophy of his life before us, we felt that the only fit custodian of his physical remains could therefore be the elements. And what place could serve better as his final resting place than the bosom of India's lakes and mighty rivers? So, sacred Triveni was chosen for the main ceremony of immersion. In its immemorial flow, it had mingled the ashes of the nameless millions of India, whose joys and sorrows he had made his own and in whose collective life it was his ambition to merge himself like a drop in the ocean.

* * *

For the last time the railway authorities ran a special train for the Mahatma—this time for his ashes.

There were dense, seething crowds at all railway stations, big and small, throughout the journey. Some had walked on foot long distances just to catch a glimpse of the fateful train. Silent and sad, they stood, tears trickling down their eyes. Some of them had waited there like that for more than 24 hours. Now and then, someone would break out into an anguished cry, calling the departed one by name, and banging his or her head against the compartment wall.

At the riverside, the urn containing the ashes was transferred from the flower-bedecked truck to a 'duck'. The amphibious landing craft sailed right into the middle of the stream where the white current of the Ganga joins the Jamuna's blue flow. For some distance, the two run side by side without mingling so as to be easily distinguishable from each other. Here, what was left of the Mahatma's mortal remains was consigned to the sacred waters at the Sangam—the confluence of the Ganga, the Jamuna and the Sarasvati, the three rivers whose names are interwoven in the web of Indian history from time immemorial. Nearly three million people witnessed the ceremony from the riverbank as, to the chanting of the Vedic hymns, the urn was emptied into the placid bosom of the river. He had "outsoared the shadow of the night" and passed from death into immortality.

The river had emptied itself into the sea.

* * *

THE DROP MERGES